the art of knitting

the art of knitting

inspirational stitches, textures and surfaces

text, photographs and diagrams by
Françoise Tellier-Loumagne

translator and consultant editor:
Sandy Black

Thames & Hudson

Translated from the French
Mailles, les mouvements du fil by Sandy Black

First published in the United Kingdom in 2005 by
Thames & Hudson Ltd, 181A High Holborn,
London WC1V 7QX

www.thamesandhudson.com

First published in 2005 in paperback
in the United States of America by
Thames & Hudson Inc., 500 Fifth Avenue,
New York, New York 10110

thamesandhudsonusa.com

Original version © 2003 Aubanel,
an imprint of Éditions Minerva, Geneva
This edition © 2005 Thames & Hudson Ltd, London

British Library Cataloguing-in-Publication Data
A catalogue record for this book is available
from the British Library

ISBN-13: 978-0-500-28557-2

ISBN-10: 0-500-28557-8

Printed and bound in France - n°L96482

Contents

Introduction

When I decided to write this book, several groups of readers naturally came to mind:

- my students, who did not have a basic textbook on knitted textiles that allowed them to be more independent.
- lecturers in the applied arts, and their varying range of skills. Many have not been trained in knitting, and do not currently have an opportunity to brush up their knowledge.
- beginners in various professional fields, who have a lot of enthusiasm but little practical experience, and who consequently put forward ideas drawn from the press, source books and stores.
- members of the general public with a growing interest in hobbies and crafts, but who are not used to creating or expressing themselves within the field of knitting in particular.
- artists and craftspeople, and all those who use yarn and textiles as a means of expression, but rarely consider working with knit.

It seemed to me that existing books in this field are often not suitable for creative designers, for several reasons:

- they generally encourage readers to copy, but not to create.
- they may be too general – in professional schools, one or two theoretical works often cover the entire textiles course. These may be clear, but are often very brief, and do not allow for diversions down untrodden paths.
- alternatively, they may be too highly specialized – this is the case for technical manuals targeted at specialists and engineers, which are difficult for creative young designers to grasp.
- finally, the literature is rapidly outdated.

Another difficulty is that there are countless possible knitting techniques, but the vocabulary used to describe them is often specific to one sector of the industry, to a particular geographical area, or to a particular period of time, and across these different fields, the same terms do not always describe the same processes, nor the same results.

With these points in mind, I decided to create a book that will try to change the way in which knitted textiles are perceived, and so encourage readers to personally express themselves. I hope it will be a work that builds a bridge between technicians and designers and vice versa, and that makes communication more 'objective' and more creative; a clear source of information that allows new pathways to innovation to be discovered.

Background

Knitting is often referred to in a pejorative manner, and stereotypically is seen as something that is only of interest to the elderly. Magazines and books dedicated exclusively to these pursuits are disappearing from news-stands and libraries, and many manufacturers of domestic knitting machines are ceasing production. Paradoxically, at the same time, an increase in free time has led to a major rise in interest in handicrafts. I also notice, every year, that in classes of young textile and fashion designers, more than three quarters of them are passionate about machine-knitting, and more recently also about hand-knitting. The hand-made look regularly returns in seasonal fashion trends; for this reason, the Parisian couture houses all maintain a network of 'makers' (who may use hand-knitting, domestic machine-knitting, crochet, embroidery or other techniques).

All across Europe, the yarn spinning industry went into decline some years ago. The regions that formerly specialized in spinning, knitted fabrics and clothing manufacture are becoming increasingly troubled: manufacturing is relocating overseas, to countries where production costs are extremely low. However, some companies still survive and are doing very well: they have built themselves a reputation for innovation, performance or the highest level of luxury, without worrying too much about price. This is the case in Italy, for yarn spinning and the whole of the sector; it is also true for the few knitwear factories remaining in France.

It must be pointed out that, while production has moved away, the creative design of many French collections is carried out mainly in Paris. Outside of the capital, however, some manufacturing companies have in-house design studios, which enable them to take an active part in the development of the new collections.

Within the industry, 'second skin' knitwear, which is light and supple, is extremely popular and frequently used in fashion and accessories. Uses for knitting can also be found in the environment, and in lesser-known sectors such as medicine (surgery, rehabilitation and nursing care), transport, packaging, maintenance and civil engineering. Progress in these areas is stunning. In fact, almost all textiles are now becoming 'technical' or 'intelligent'. For example, they may be breathable, water-repellant, thermo-regulating or moisture regulating, haemostatic, reflective, optical, thermochromic, acoustic, perfumed, anti-bacterial or anti-UV.

It is notable, however, that the discrepancy has increased between, on the one hand, the increasing capabilities of the production equipment, and on the other, the very basic nature of many designs. In fact, production hardware is increasingly high-performance: the newest knitwear is now made in three dimensions, meaning without seams, and often includes complex details (such as edgings or pockets). Knitting is no longer created just lengthways but in all directions; structures are becoming more and more complex, using an impressive number of yarns in the same course to make textured relief patterns; fabrics can now be transparent, stretchy, comfortable or lightweight.

But who is buying these machines? Factory owners in Europe are disappearing, and as in the computer industry, the equipment is very expensive and rapidly becomes obsolete. And who programmes these machines? In the most cases only the machine builders themselves are able to do this, and so it is the engineers who develop the prototypes, incorporating the newest technical capabilities, and not textile or fashion designers nor design studios, who generally suggest ideas that are

already commonplace. Some sectors, such as the luxury goods industry, have their own specialist programmers, because their short production cycles do not allow enough manufacturing time to sub-contract this task.

Industrial knitting machines are exceedingly complex, expensive, cumbersome and heavy, and so are more rarely found in art and design college workshops. In addition, there are countless different models that are all to some extent adapted to a specific type of manufacturing. Within education, students are encouraged to use all types of hand craft techniques, old and new, but consequently, they are not always in a position to explain their concepts in a way that the industry will understand.

But how do we resolve all these contradictions? Quite clearly it is impossible to turn every art student into a technician or engineer, on top of their already demanding education. How do we rectify the lack of qualified and motivated technicians? And how do we make knitting more dynamic within the fields of leisure, craftwork and art?

Perhaps one way is to raise awareness among the media and the potential audience by means of exhibitions and training courses, by creating connections and synergies at all levels. Some yarn companies welcome hand-knitting customers, and the knitting industry is apparently interested in training. They organize competitions, offer yarn samples, and distribute swatches knitted on industrial machines to the colleges at no cost, along with their technical specifications. On the educational side, colleges arrange industrial visits to companies, student placements, and partnerships on specific projects. These initiatives are still insufficient, and must be promoted and followed through. However, they must also be carefully monitored, because some sectors of the industry are so used to having a free source of ongoing design help that it poses a serious ethical problem! To improve this situation, it is crucial to pass on the desire to learn and practice; to allow different methods of manufacture to be compared, and so encourage technical specialists, designers, visual artists and creative craftspeople to

come together to experiment. There must also be passion (not to mention patience) at all levels, inside and outside of the industry; none of the time spent on training, research, creation of ideas, and manufacture is worth anything without it.

Approach and structure

In view of this complex situation, this book aims to explore other potential approaches. This is primarily an attempt to change the usual viewpoint, to demonstrate the many different types of stitches that are possible in knitting, and to suggest ways of exploring and experimenting with these.

I have chosen a basic theme for the book that is well known but infinitely varied, and potentially appealing to a wide audience – the natural textures of the earth and the changing seasons. This will form a pretext for looking at colours and materials, the way in which they change with light and shade, and for playing ambiguously with the textures of different weft-knitting structures. The themed images are not intended to be exhaustive, nor are they all illustrated by knitted samples; they simply suggest directions that those inspired to do their own research may wish to explore.

Coming up with a classification system was not a simple task; the resulting order is somewhat arbitrary. It gives precedence to the capabilities of hand frame machines over those of industrial machines and of hand-knitting. The more experienced are invited to draw freely from the book, and beginners are encouraged to follow up the basics learned from their instruction manuals by experimenting and adding information chapter by chapter. And in every case, this can be combined with a personal theme, a subject, a style or an idea.

I would strongly recommend that all training on industrial knitting machinery is combined with training in the skills of hand-knitting. While on knitting machines, the action of the needles is hidden by the carriage, knitting by hand allows each stage of the operation to be observed. In addition, the processes used to create stitches are often very different. While this may cause some confusion at

first, it also encourages a creative attitude towards technical details, and nurtures the ability to envisage different ways of creating the same or similar results. These qualities are important, especially in the business world, when it comes to tackling production issues and adapting collections to take into account the capabilities and limitations of different machines. Also, the ability to modify a project while preserving its major selling points can have a beneficial effect on other areas, such as production costs.

Training must allow factual knowledge to be acquired, but it should also pass on research skills that are based primarily on experimentation: observation, analysis, and deduction. For example, after producing a sample (whether or not it was successful), it is important to ask yourself what could be improved, left out, or combined with other ideas. Often the first trials do not produce anything really interesting, but they can be reworked into later samples. Although producing stunning results by accident in a single step is not impossible, it is nonetheless very rare. However, minor mistakes and even major disasters can often be turned around and transformed into new opportunities.

Topics covered

• An introductory section that describes basic textile concepts, the specifics of weft knitting and warp knitting, and the materials used.

• Seventeen chapters that illustrate the range of possible fabric structures in weft knitting: plain knitting, openwork knitting (with float stitches), creative knitting (stitches made by research and experimentation), multiple knits or stitches using many colours on a single-bed machine, slipped stitches made with held loops, tuck stitches, purl fabrics using stitches in relief, tubular knitting, ribs, racked stitches, transferred stitches, some variations on different transfer structures, jacquards knitted in several colours on double-bed machines, and some special effects (pile and fake fur fabrics).

At the beginning of each chapter, a deliberately ambiguous image shows the knit structure integrated into natural surroundings, often echoing its form and construction. Next, the principle behind each stitch or fabric is formally described; each is accompanied by two greatly enlarged images of the face and reverse of the fabric, a knitted sample, a schematic and technical diagram, and examples showing the basic variations and their special characteristics. Some of the samples used echo the themes from previous chapters. The overall design tries to maintain the theme of each chapter, while paying close attention to the sensual qualities of materials, colours and textures. In contrast to most literature on knitting, detailed explanations of the stitch variations are deliberately not included, to encourage readers to take a questioning approach and carry out research of their own.

• A conclusion that examines the probable evolution of weft knitting.

• An appendix that explains the basics of knitted textiles and methods of notation.

• A glossary that gives definitions for the basic technical terminology.

Basics

1 Textiles

Textiles are surfaces and volumes made out of yarns, fibres or filaments, which may be intermeshed together in a variety of different ways. They can be divided as follows:

- fabrics in which the yarns intermesh in two or more directions, such as weaving, tapestry, gauze, tulle, lace, basketry or braiding.
- fabrics structured from a series of loops, such as weft knitting and warp knitting.
- fabrics in which fibrous materials are entangled, melted, or bonded together: non-wovens made from batts of fibres or filaments held together by needlepunching, felting, bonding, pressing or heat-setting.
- complex fabrics made using multiple techniques, such as tufted, woven, knitted and non-woven fabrics bonded or sewn together with one or more other textiles, or coated fabrics.

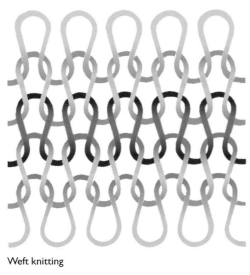

Weft knitting

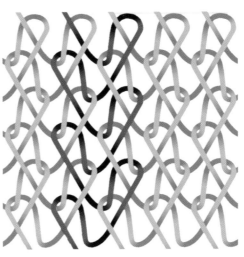

Warp knitting

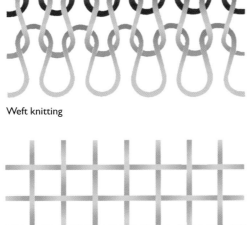

Weaving

Inlaid warp knitting

2 Weft knitting and warp knitting

There are two very different techniques for creating fabrics from intermeshed loops: weft knitting and warp knitting.

Weft-knitted fabrics are created from one yarn whose loops link together in successive courses throughout the length. This construction allows very flexible items to be produced, which can be stretched and shaped even if the yarn used is not itself stretchy. The huge potential for producing different samples with weft knitting is explored in this book. In the weft-knitting process, the yarns within the different stitch structures move relatively easily, which enables the knitted textile to be distorted in any direction. This technique is therefore frequently used in clothing, especially for underwear, lingerie and sportswear, which has become increasingly responsive to performance requirements under extreme conditions.

The very diverse scope of knitwear production requires the use of a wide range of machinery, much of which is highly specialized.

Warp-knitted fabrics are created from the knitting of a number of different yarns wound onto a beam (as in weaving). These yarns form chains of loops along the length of the fabric, which are also linked together laterally in a wide variety of ways. In contrast to weft knitting, warp-knitted fabrics are very difficult to unravel. They are generally much less flexible, like woven fabrics. These textiles can incorporate an impressive number of colours and different fancy yarns (as many as the number of warp chains!). The resulting textiles can be extremely varied in appearance and may incorporate relief effects, openwork, weft insertions and loops, among other features. Brands of warp-knitting machinery include Raschel, Murata and Simplex. Unfortunately for the manufacturing process and for designers, sampling warp-knitted fabrics is not practical on anything other than industrial machines.

Because of the constraints of manufacturing (the time taken to prepare the warp beam), but also because of their many possible characteristics, warp-knitted fabrics are frequently used in the household sector (net curtains, bedspreads, upholstery, furnishing trimmings), for accessories (bags, belts, hats), in the technical sector for items such as packaging for fruit and vegetables, and for nets of all sorts. Warp knitting is also found in the clothing field, in items such as fine lingerie, swimwear and lace.

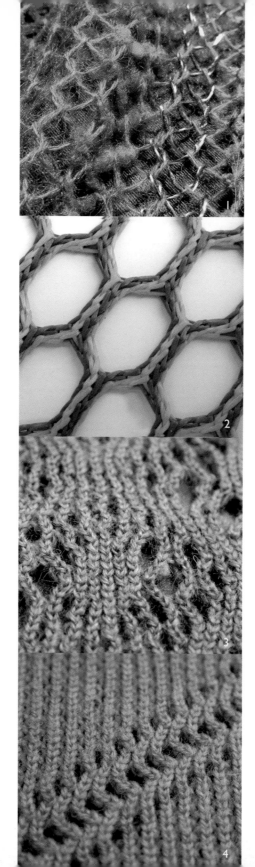

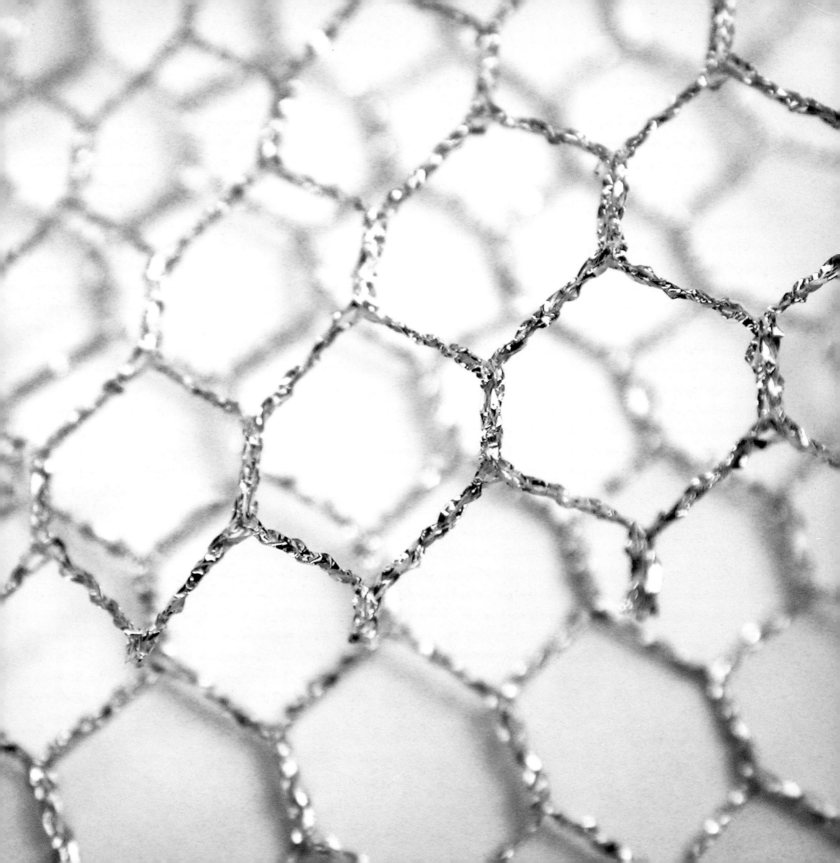

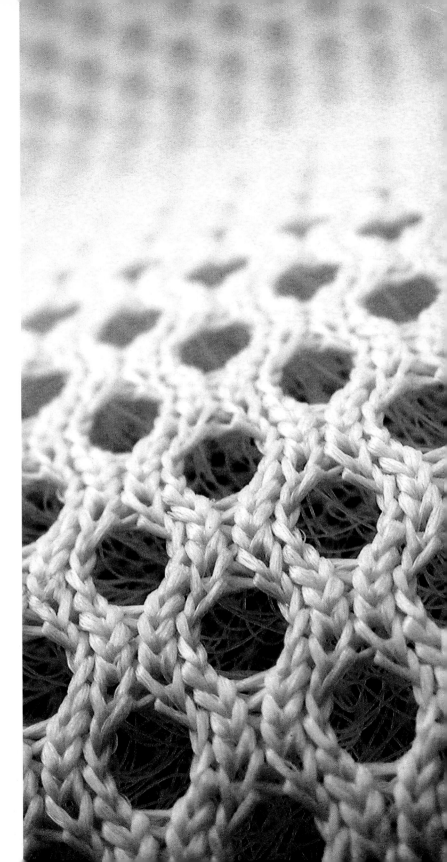

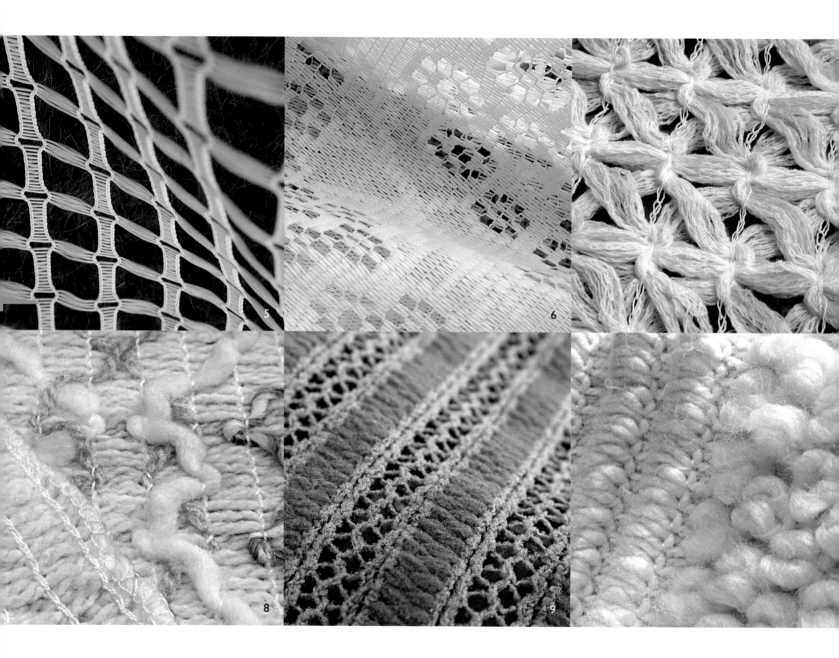

3 Materials

Textiles of natural origin

These are obtained by physical and mechanical transformation of natural fibres without altering their composition.

Textiles of plant origin

These are made from fibres found in the flowers, seeds, stems, and leaves of plants: cotton, kapok, linen, hemp, jute, ramie, sisal, coconut, or even sap, as in rubber.

Textiles of animal origin

These are made from the hair of animals, including sheep (wool), goat (mohair, cashmere), rabbit (angora), camel, llama, vicuna and alpaca, or from the secretions of insects, such as silkworms or spiders (silk).

Textiles of mineral origin

These may be made from substances including asbestos, metals and peat.

Textiles of chemical origin

Artificial and synthetic textiles are obtained by chemical transformations and processes of varying complexity, using base materials that may be of plant, animal or mineral (petroleum) origin. A first-level transformation could produce viscose, acetate, glass fibre, metallic yarns or laminated metallic yarns, for example. More complex transformations are used to produce polyamide, polyester, acrylic, polyurethane or polyolefin.

The fibres may be either short or long, very fine or very thick, smooth or fluffy, matt or shiny, transparent or opaque, bulky or compact, very fluid or lively, stretch or non-stretch; they may now even be optical, reflective, acoustic, or perfumed. They may be used both as a single material or combined with others. The cross-section of the fibre may vary a great deal in dimensions and shape (circular, flat, or cross, for example), and new structures are constantly being created, improving the fibre's qualities of drape, weight, appearance and touch, its wicking ability and breathability.

4 Yarns

The textile industry, and knitwear in particular, uses yarns that can range from the subtle to the extravagant. This is apparent even in the vocabulary used to describe them. Plain yarns may be singles, folded or plied, cabled or gimped, while fancy yarns may be bouclé, chenille, crepe, coated, crimped, fleck, frisée, gimp, irisé, jaspé, nep, knopped, loop, printed, marl, wavy, pearlized, slub, snarl, space dyed or variegated.

The appearance of a yarn depends on the type of fibre and its method of manufacture (twisting, bonding, spinning, fibre mixing, weaving, knitting) as well as finishing treatments or embellishments (dyeing, mercerizing, printing, coating).

The fibre content and structure of a yarn is crucial to the form and rhythm it will create when knitted. In some cases, however, the clarity of the stitch structure disappears totally beneath the texture of the yarn and fibre used. The behaviour of yarns must be carefully taken into account when selecting suitable stitch structures for textiles.

Like lines and brushstrokes in painting, yarns have life, memory and expression. They can also be understood in a subjective manner: some yarns seem arrogant, rebellious and wild; others are obedient and straightforward. They may be shy, pretentious, sophisticated or perhaps witty. They can even be carefree and sexy. Some may be robust, lively, playful, and others rough, austere and taciturn, or even nostalgic.

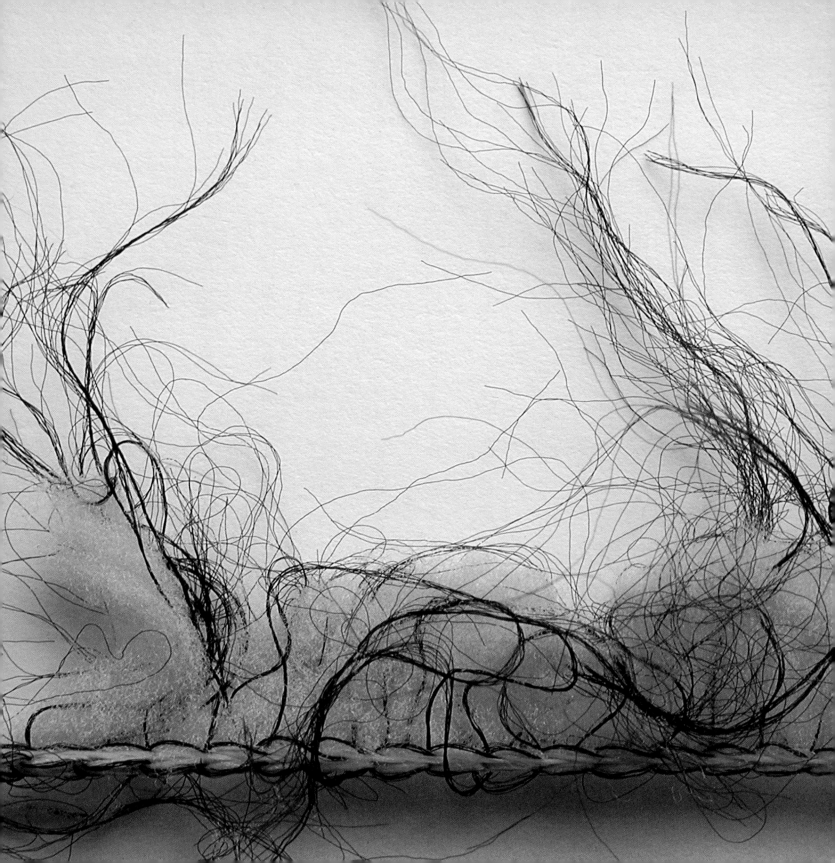

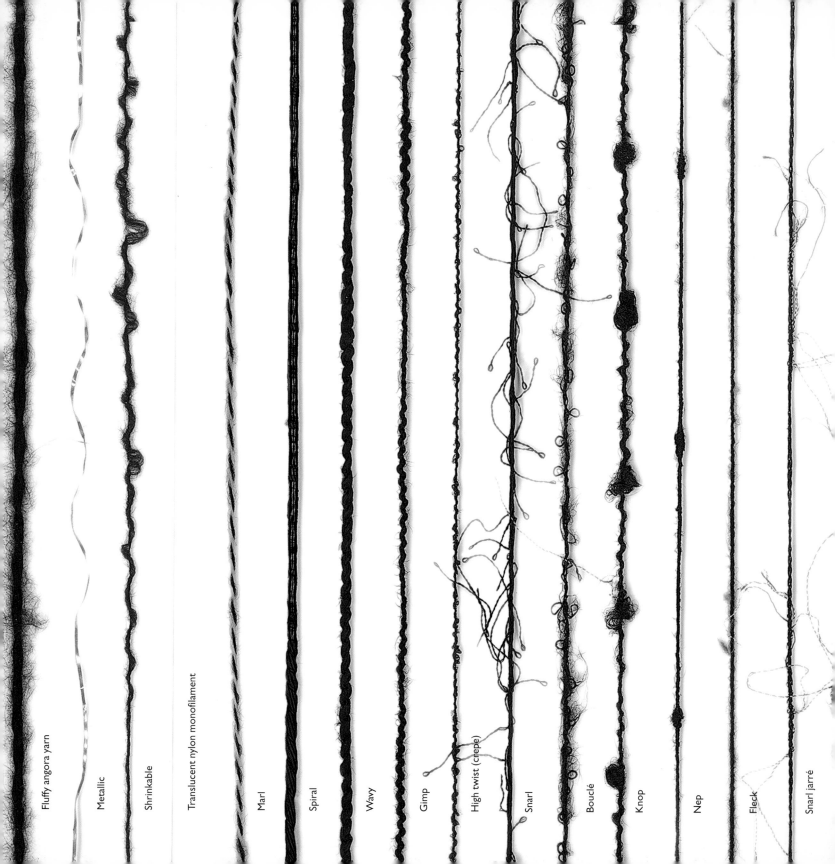

Fluffy angora yarn

Metallic

Shrinkable

Translucent nylon monofilament

Marl

Spiral

Wavy

Gimp

High twist (crepe)

Snarl

Bouclé

Knop

Nep

Fleck

Snarl jarré

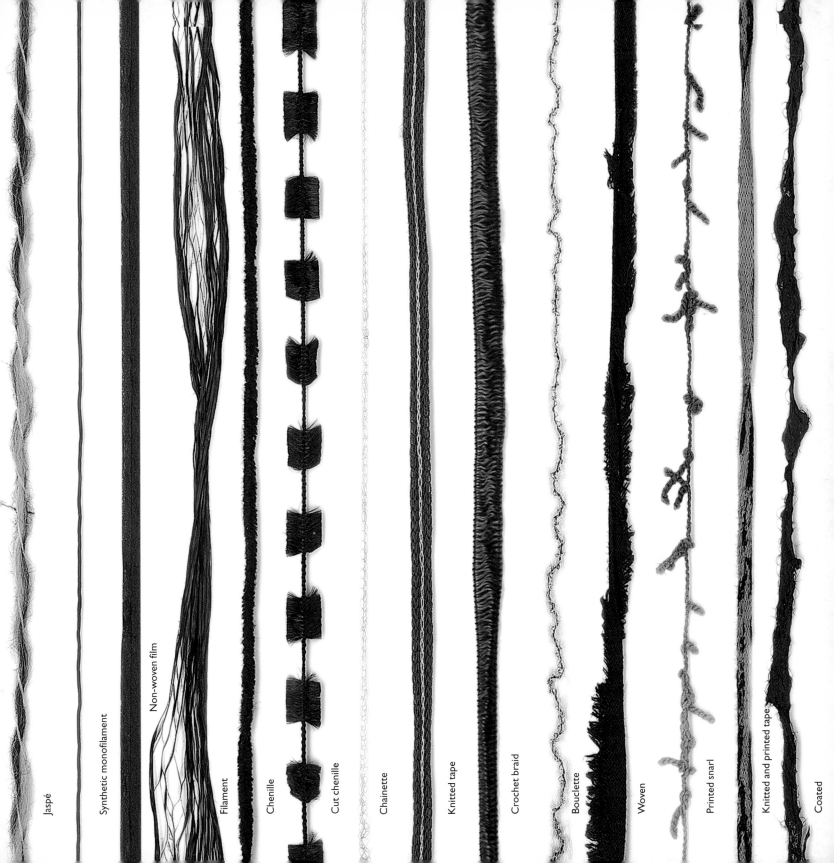

Jaspé

Synthetic monofilament

Non-woven film

Filament

Chenille

Cut chenille

Chainette

Knitted tape

Crochet braid

Bouclette

Woven

Printed snarl

Knitted and printed tape

Coated

Weft knitting:
stitches and structures

1 Basic stitches: single jersey or plain knitting

Knitted fabrics consisting entirely of the basic knit loop repeated throughout the whole fabric are termed single jersey, plain fabric, stockinette or, in hand-knitting, stocking stitch. This is the most basic structure in weft knitting. Jersey is also a generic term often used to denote fabrics industrially knitted in very fine gauge, both plain and textured.

On the right side or face (knit side) of the fabric, the legs of the stitches are visible, forming a series of V-shapes repeated horizontally and vertically. On the reverse side (purl side), the foot and head of the stitch loops appear in relief, forming wavy horizontal lines that repeat for the entire length.

The path taken by the yarn as it forms the stitches creates one of the characteristics of weft knitting and particularly of single jersey fabric: it rolls at the edges, to the reverse (purl) side in the direction parallel to the wales, and to the face (knit) side in the direction parallel to the courses. When single jersey is left unfinished (and not pressed), a range of results can be obtained; these include rouleau finishes, individual 'frills' with rolled edges that can be applied in bands, and specialist textiles such as absorbent wipes.

The look of single jersey varies according to the fibre, form, texture and count of the yarn used; the machine gauge, the stitch length settings of the carriage, and the treatments and finishes applied to the final knitted fabric. Some fabrics are more interesting on the reverse than the face, such as those knitted from highly textured yarns with pronounced textural effects such as knops – these remain on the reverse side, as they are difficult to knit through the loops of the previous course.

Because it is cheap to produce, single jersey and its variations account for a large proportion of industrial production. It is knitted on single-bed flat knitting machines, or as tubular single jersey on double-bed flat machines and circular machines.

In hand-knitting, knitting the stitches of every course creates the basic fabric called garter stitch (see chapter 7). As the knitting is turned at the end of every course, the loops intermesh in the opposite direction each time. To obtain single jersey (stocking stitch) manually on two needles, it is necessary to knit the stitches on the face (right side), and purl on the reverse (wrong side). Single jersey is therefore the second basic fabric learned in hand-knitting, not the first, in contrast to machine-knitting.

Single-bed jersey

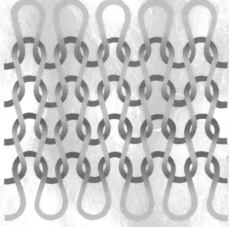

Jersey right side (face)

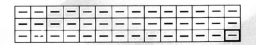

Tubular jersey

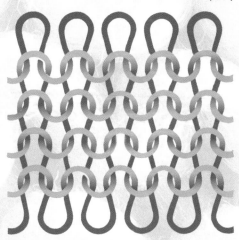

Jersey wrong side (reverse)

Treatments and embellishments

Some treatments and finishes are intended to improve the technical quality of the knitting, and have little effect on its appearance, but do affect the feel of the fabric to a lesser or greater extent. This is the case for antistatic, anti-pilling, crease-resistant, non-shrinking, non-felting, waterproofing, water-repellent, flame-retardant, moth-proofing, and stain- resistant treatments, for instance. Unfortunately, these treatments are not always completely effective!

Other finishes can change the appearance of the textile, and some totally mask the structure of the stitches. These include pressing, dyeing, brushing, shearing, felting, flocking, coating, various types of printing (such as devoré, which burns away one of the component fibres of the yarn, leaving a transparent pattern on an opaque ground), embroidery, bonding and needlepunching.

A number of effects can be obtained manually on a small scale. Experimentation with a range of sometimes unconventional methods can lead to the discovery of interesting and unusual effects.

Plating

Plated knitting has two sides, each with a different appearance: for instance, plain and mixed colour, matt and shiny, light and dark. The knitting is made using two different yarns together, one being visible on the face side, the other on the reverse. On domestic machines, this is achieved by changing the yarn feeder (which on these machines is a removable part fitted onto the carriage). On industrial machines, a plating feeder is used (also removable). The two yarns are thus precisely guided during the knitting, and kept one in front of the other. Recently, many elasticated fabrics have appeared, plated with an 'invisible' elastane yarn. In hand-knitting, this precision is practically impossible to achieve.

Stripes

As knitting consists of the accumulation of successive courses, alternating different yarns (in colour, form, texture, weight, fibre) and varying the stitch tension setting creates horizontal patterns of stripes.

24

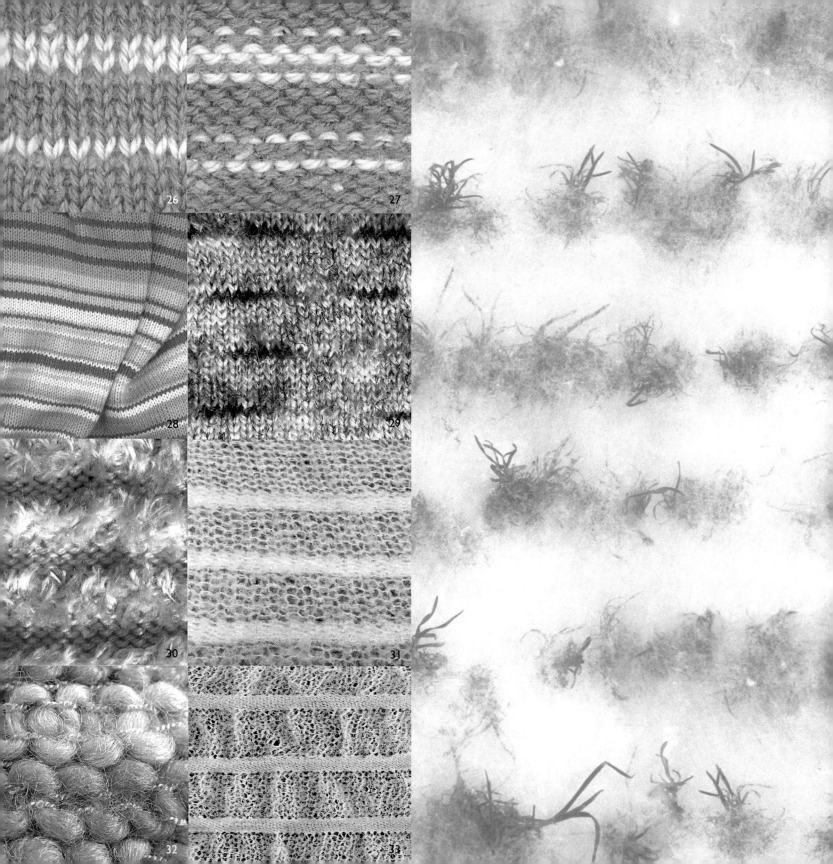

26

27

28

29

30

31

32

33

34

35

36

37

38

39

40

41

Plated knitting made using contrast yarns can be striped by alternating the position of the two yarns in the plating feeder.

Recent industrial machines produce striped patterns without any difficulty. On domestic machines, which have only one yarn feeder (i.e. a single knitting system and single yarn guide), the changing of yarns can only be done automatically every two courses, or another even number. In order to work with stripes made up of odd numbers of courses, great care must be taken to knit 'empty' traverses with the carriage set 'out of action' or 'slip', and to cut the yarn when necessary.

In hand-knitting, the use of double-pointed needles makes striping with odd numbers of rows easier, without having to cut the yarn. These allow the knitting to be easily worked from either left to right, or right to left.

Some examples showing different effects in jersey.

Variations in texture according to the yarns used:
Page 41 – reverse jersey made with a fancy yarn.
Page 42
1 – Reverse jersey made with an irregular yarn.
2 – Reverse jersey made with a covered yarn.
3 – Plain jersey made with a chenille yarn.
4 – Reverse jersey made with a loop yarn: the texture of the yarn totally hides the structure of the stitches.
5 – Reverse jersey made with a chenille yarn.
6 – Plain jersey made with a slub yarn.
7 – Reverse jersey made with a knopped yarn.
8 – Plain jersey knitted with an irregular stitch length.
Variations in texture and appearance created by changing the stitch length setting – 2, 5, 8.

Some examples of finishing treatments:
Page 43 – brushing, plain knit side
Page 45
9 – Cornely embroidery: chain stitch
10, 12 – Embroidery
11 – Embroidery with an elastic thread
13 – Applied sequins
14, 15 – Printing
16 – Flocking
17 – Devoré printing
18 – Coating
19 – Coated knitting embroidered onto a jersey fabric backing containing Lycra; on steaming the jersey backing contracts, creating a textural effect on the coated surface.
20 – Pleating
21 – Bonded sequins
22 – Heat bonding
23 – Shape forming by heat setting

Pages 46–47 – Plating: examples created by varying the characteristics of the two yarns used (tone, colour, fibres, textures, count), either similar or highly contrasting.
24 – Reverse jersey side, white knops appearing on grey ground; plain jersey side, the fine grey yarn does not show.
25 – Plain jersey side, marl effect, reverse jersey side single colour.

Page 48 – Stripes
26, 27 – Contrast tones: one course, then two courses of lighter yarn on a dark ground, face and reverse.
28 – Contrast of tones and colour with regular and irregular rhythm.
29 – Ikat effect or intermittent stripes produced by a printed yarn.
30 – Textural effect made with a chenille yarn.
Opaque and transparent effects:
31 – Fabric knitted from one yarn, but alternately doubled.
32 – Knitting using two yarns with very different counts.
33 – Knitting using a shrinkable yarn; after steaming, the areas knitted with another yarn pucker up.
Page 49
34, 35, 36, 37 – Stripes created by changing the stitch length setting at either regularly or random intervals.
38, 39 – Plated stripes face and reverse.
40, 41 – Plated and plain stripes, face and reverse.
Page 50 – Use of rolled edges of jersey: seams and novelty scarves.

2 Knitting with 'absent' stitches

Openwork (or 'needle-out') knitting

Light and transparent nets made with fine yarns and giant stitches, here referred to as openwork stitches, look as if they have been made on a very large gauge machine. The effect is created on a normal machine, by casting on only every second, third or more needle.

Another method is, after knitting, to drop every second or third (or more) stitch and allow it to ladder the full length of the fabric. The result is almost the same, but slightly irregular, like hand-knitting.

By hand, openwork fabrics can be obtained in several ways: by using needles much larger than normally recommended for the yarn and structure; by wrapping the yarn round the needle two or three times between stitches; or letting stitches drop and ladder down to the cast-on edge.

Float stitches

These are transparent knits incorporating floats built up horizontally, in which some of the needles have been 'missed' or left out of action. Either some needles are not selected during casting on, or stitches are dropped during knitting.

In single jersey, if the yarn is fluid and smooth, and the tension setting is loosened, the ladder will run extremely easily; in other cases, or if the knitting is fixed by pressing, coating or another finishing treatment, the floats and stitches will hold their position.

Stranded fabrics and fringes

Stranded fabrics consisting of large floats are obtained by missing out all needles except the selvedge needles during cast on, or by dropping all stitches after knitting. They can be used in many ways – as fringes or stripes, or bonded, felted, coated or embroidered onto a supporting fabric (which may or may not be cut or washed away).

When working with very few needles, it is also possible to bring more needles into action. Attention is required, however, because if two adjacent needles are put back into action, then only one enlarged stitch will be formed, not two. This operation also carries the risk of crashing the needles (if they are in the wrong position) or entangling the yarn in the brushes of the carriage. To avoid this, the same method as increasing should be used – only bringing into action one single needle at a time between two already knitting. The positioning of the needles creates the final effect.

In hand-knitting, these effects can be obtained in the same manner as for openwork, such as dropping the stitches and laddering back to the cast-on edge.

Drop-stitch fabrics

These are often created only too easily by beginners! If a loop escapes from the needle, the entire column of stitches unravels, with a speed that depends on the fibre used and the tension setting. In order to preserve an interesting but ephemeral drop-stitch design, a suitable finishing treatment must be used. A stitch that has run can be retrieved by re-knitting manually using a crochet hook or latch tool (see illustration, page 298).

Sometimes, stitches are deliberately dropped during knitting to create a pattern. There is a clever technique for stabilizing the stitches in this case: first create a very tight course, then another extremely loose one, then drop the selected pattern stitches either singly or in groups. Single jersey fabrics roll, and the dropped loops will curl towards the knit side. These fabrics look both dense and open in parts, similar in appearance to crochet lace.

If the empty needles remain 'out of action', this creates floats on the following courses.

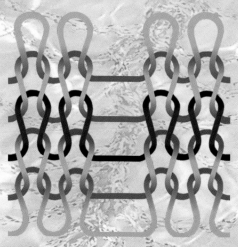

Float stitches, right side

Reverse

To put needles back in action:

- for individual stitches, all that is needed is to move the empty needle to working position B or C (see pp. 293–94 for needle positions).
- for two or more needles together, in order to obtain plain fabric, the method is the same as casting on, in two stages: push the needles to knitting position, pass the carriage to knit a course, push these needles to position D, and with a latch-tool, twist the float from the previous course around each needle, making separate loops, then knit the next course. As in these circumstances the fabric is not weighted, it is necessary to push the needles to position D for several courses more.

It is also possible to create different effects by progressively knitting in needles on each course, pushing up one needle between two already knitting each time. The main problem with these structures is the risk of accidentally dropping stitches.

In hand-knitting, drop-stitch patterns are difficult to create. The manipulations tend to encourage stitches to run. Casting on is done in two steps: in the first row, wrap the yarn once or more around the needle, then on the following row, knit one then purl one into the float, and so on.

Cast-off stitch patterning

As in drop-stitch patterning, this method enables decorative holes to be created in the fabric without the risk of unravelling. Unlike earlier industrial knitting machines, more recent ones can cast off and cast on stitches anywhere within the knitted fabric.

To obtain similar effects on a domestic machine, the course must be knitted manually in parts, and stitches cast off where needed: (*) using a latch tool, pick up a stitch, transfer a loop to the next needle, pass both loops behind the latch, place the yarn in the hook, and knit the two loops together (*), then repeat from (*) to (*). Use the method described in the previous paragraph to put needles back into knitting after casting off.

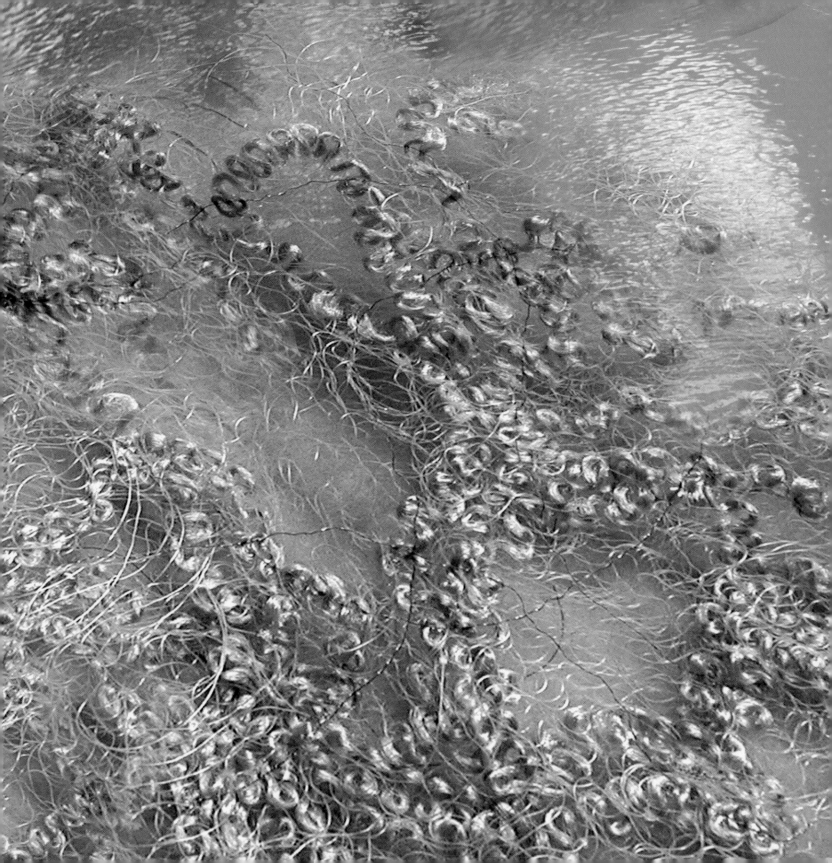

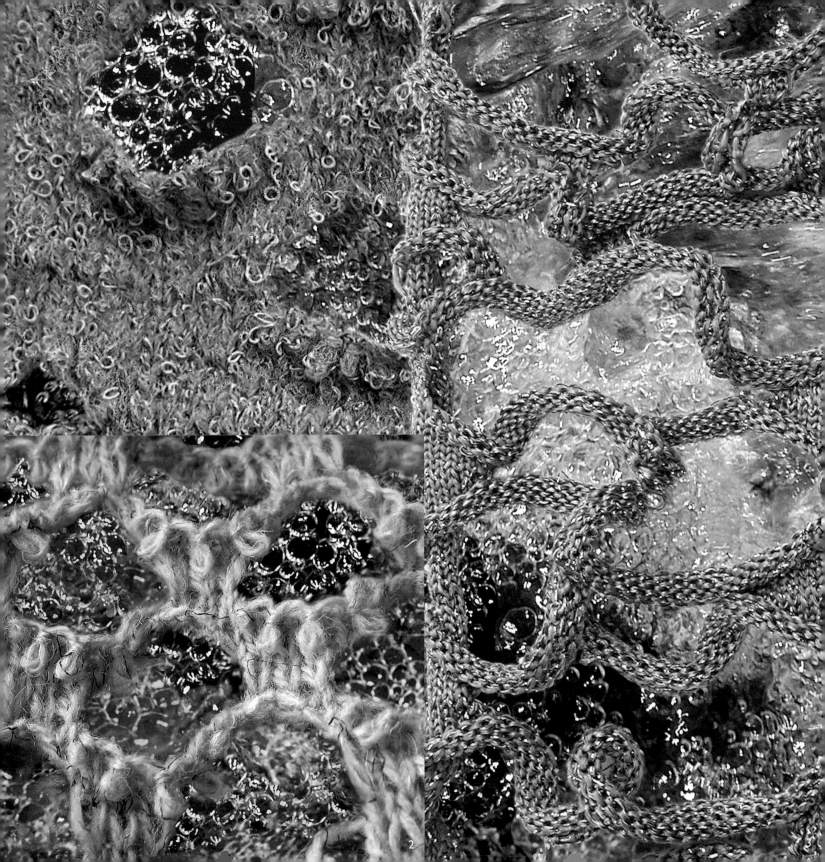

3 Experimental and creative stitches

I have included in this chapter all structures obtained by experimental manipulation. With a little experience, and a great deal of observation, creativity and sensitivity, it is possible to create an enormous number of attractive and often innovative samples, especially by hand-tooling on various backgrounds of plain or striped jersey, openwork, and so on. Stitches can be transferred to left or right, others picked up from the knitting below and put back on the needles to be knitted again, forming puckers, regular or irregular ripples, and transparent or opaque effects. This experimental stage is important in order to become accustomed to different materials, to understand the specific characteristics of the yarns, to evaluate the tension settings, and to learn to analyse, select, and emphasize or reduce the effects obtained. This experimentation is also useful because it balances the inevitable frustrations of learning to knit with moments of pleasure and success. The majority of structures can in any case now be reproduced industrially (but using other methods!).

In contrast, in hand-knitting it is better to learn to recognize the stitches, master their variety, and know how to count the rows before beginning to take risks, as beginners generally do not understand their mistakes and so cannot make the most of them.

Page 69

1 – Spider's web effects are obtained with very few
needles in action: the wales become closer or further
apart according to the manual positioning of the
stitches using the latch tool.

2 – Regular or irregular puckers and ripples are
obtained using the latch tool by picking up the heads of
the stitches from a previous course. For regular three-
dimensional effects it is better to use a marker that
may or may not be temporary: at the chosen position,
knit a course with an additional fine, smooth and
strong thread, then several courses later, pick up the
marked loops. When the knitting is finished pull the
supplementary thread out. Here, the yarn is space-
dyed with several colours.

3– The same process with a print.

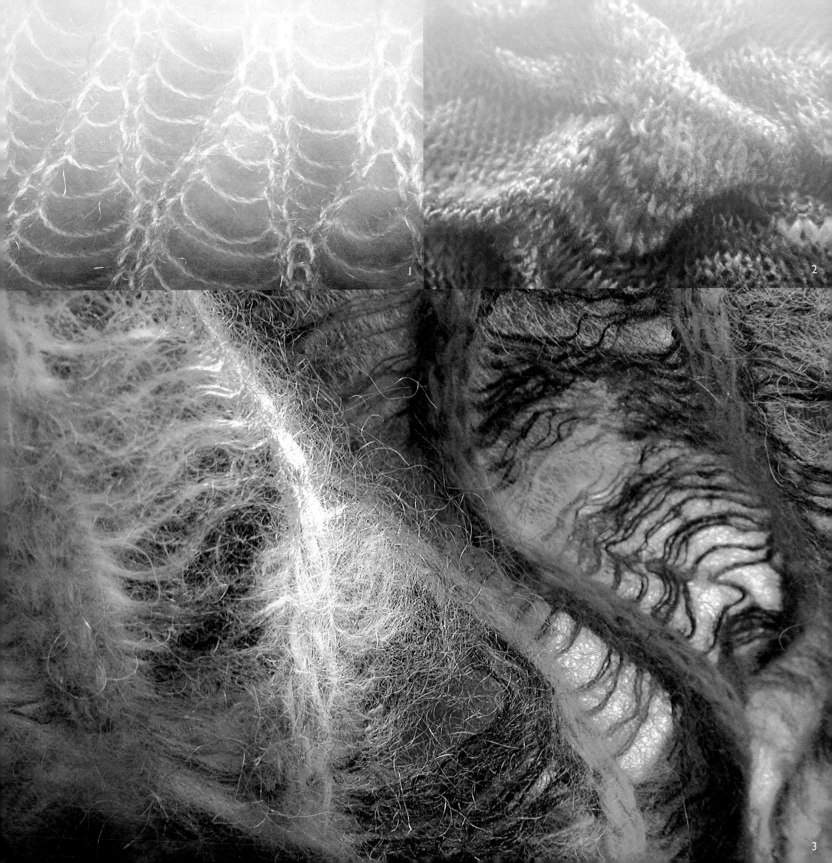

1

2

3

4 'Multiple' stitches: jacquard

In knitting, the term 'jacquard' can be used to refer to anything other than plain or horizontally striped fabrics. Vertical or diagonal stripes, checks or any other simple or complex designs all require needle selection, whether manual, mechanical or electronic. The design may have different textures (float or slip stitch, tuck stitch, purl stitches), in which case it is a structured jacquard (also known as structured stitches). When it has several different yarns (fibres, yarn count, colour), it is referred to as a colour jacquard.

Jacquard designs are developed on computer. New software applications intended for fashion design studios can be used to simulate the stitches with their fibres and even entire garments fitted or worn on a model. In factories, the sampling of patterns is done directly on the knitting machine with the appropriate yarn. For designers, a knowledge of jacquard techniques and of sampling is always essential, both for understanding and for innovating.

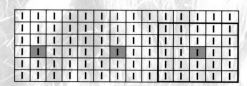

Design of two colours per course

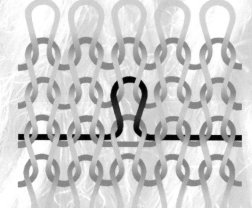

Right side

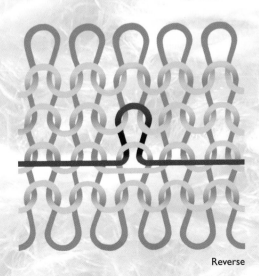

Reverse

In the case of the stitches studied in the previous chapters, the designs were obtained manually using a latch tool, whereas in industry all these structures are of course programmed. On domestic machines, programming the rear bed considerably widens the range of possible samples, although it does not completely eliminate the need for additional manual operations.

A design needs to be transposed onto squared paper, to form a chart. As the proportions of a stitch are variable and rarely square, in order to avoid major unwanted distortions, it is preferable to use specially designed grids with boxes that are slightly elongated. If greater accuracy is required, the stitch ratio must be specified; this is done by making up a sample with the correct settings and yarns, and then measuring how many stitches and courses there are in ten square centimetres (four square inches) and drawing up the grid accordingly.

Colour (or contrast fibre) jacquards are fabrics that include courses of stitches formed from two or more different yarns. The most important technical factor is in the number of colours per course and not the total number of colours of the jacquard pattern. On a single-bed machine, several methods exist for producing very different textiles: jacquard with floats, 'fishnet' stitches and intarsia. The sections that follow also show jacquards made with tuck stitches and jacquards made with slipped stitches, i.e. stitches held over a number of different courses, according to their position.

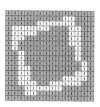
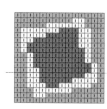
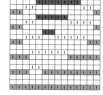

Design of two
colours per course

Chart

Design of three
colours per course

Chart

See text opposite for explanation.

Float jacquard or single jersey jacquard

On the face (knit side) of the single jersey fabric, the two-colour (common) or three or four different colour (rare) knitted loops of the same course alternate according to the design. On the reverse, the yarns that do not knit, float.

This jacquard has a hand-knitted appearance. The stitches are not distorted as in some jacquards on a double-bed machine. With two colours per course, the fabric is supple and quite light, but the weight and thickness increase significantly when knitting with one or two additional yarns throughout the entire fabric.

The yarns used to make jacquards may show colour contrasts as well as fibre, texture or yarn count. The designs can be enlivened by missing out some needles and wales. Some designs with short floats are used on the reverse (purl) side to produce a woven effect. Frequently used compositions are all-over repeats or stripes as seen in the ethnically inspired designs that regularly come back into fashion.

By shortening the length of the floats the risk of catching can be reduced, and this must therefore be taken into account in the design. Some industrial machines have a system for picking up the floats at intervals and knitting them in such a way that they do not appear on the right side. This operation can be performed manually on domestic machines by specifically lifting up the floating yarns onto a series of needles by means of a latch tool.

In some cases, particularly in hosiery, the floats are then cut away. The yarns cut off in this way can easily escape and run, but fine knitting is often made with elastomeric yarn, which limits the risk of laddering. In other cases, additional treatment (felting, printing, coating, laminating) may eliminate this drawback entirely and open the way for innovative textiles.

On domestic machines, the designs can be from two to one hundred or two hundred stitches (depending on the number of needles on the machine) and from one to an infinite number of courses. They can be repeated as all-over patterns. In this case, it is necessary to ensure that the repeat is maintained (see diagram). The design can also be positioned as a single motif or spaced regularly or irregularly over a plain coloured (or striped) jersey background by modifying the programme data. By changing the variables, the same design can also be doubled, inverted or have its colours reversed.

In a jacquard with two colours per course, each cell of the two-colour chart corresponds to one stitch, but in a jacquard of three or more colours the transposition of the design is broken down colour by colour. For three colours, one knitted course corresponds to three rows on the chart, i.e. one colour per row (see diagram, page 74).

Domestic machines generally have the facility to knit with two colours at the same time, in one single passage of the carriage, though they only possess a single yarn carrier (feeder) and, therefore, the yarn can only be changed automatically every two courses. For three- or four-colour jacquards, the carriage moves in the 'slip' position with one single yarn at a time; if an automatic colour changer is used, each yarn is knitted for two traverses, across and back, i.e. two courses at a time.

In hand-knitting, jacquards must be knitted with an efficient method to avoid the risk of yarns becoming entangled. It is also important to avoid over-tightening the knitting, as beginners are often prone to do.

'Fishnet' or thread lace jacquard

On a single-bed machine, 'partial plating' (knitting with two different yarns simultaneously — see chapter 1) is obtained by programming a design. The non-selected needles knit by taking up both yarns at the same time. The selected needles knit only the additional yarn; the other yarn floats on the reverse of the fabric. These textiles can be used on the face (knit) side of the jersey or on the reverse. Their appearance varies in particular according to the yarns used (whether similar or different fibres and yarn count) and the length of the floats. For example:

- lace effects are obtained in this way by using simultaneously a very fine transparent yarn and a thicker opaque yarn. This method is used mainly in fine gauge fabrics in the lingerie and hosiery sectors. The designs generally include short floats and the effect produced gives the impression that the knit loops are about to unravel.
- if at least one of the yarns is elastomeric, the floats can be long and slit or cut without risk.

Some domestic machines designed for jacquard knitting may have a mechanical setting that enables these effects to be obtained.

Intarsia

This technique is used to juxtapose several yarns in the same course without the drawback of floats. Each area of colour is supplied by a different yarn, which is distributed by a mobile yarn guide. There can be as many areas (or fields) as there are yarn carriers (Caperdoni machines can use up to forty-five yarns in one course). Where two different colours meet, the yarns are, in principle, crossed on the reverse side so as to avoid holes appearing. However, interesting effects can be achieved by intentionally not crossing the yarns.

Left: Fishnet jacquard
9, 11 – Jacquard face/reverse
10, 12 – Fishnet jacquard face (knit) side and reverse (float). The intentionally long floats can be cut (without risk of running).
13 – Jacquard made with 'invisible' nylon yarn: the stitches look as if they are about to unravel.
14 – Jacquard (knit side)

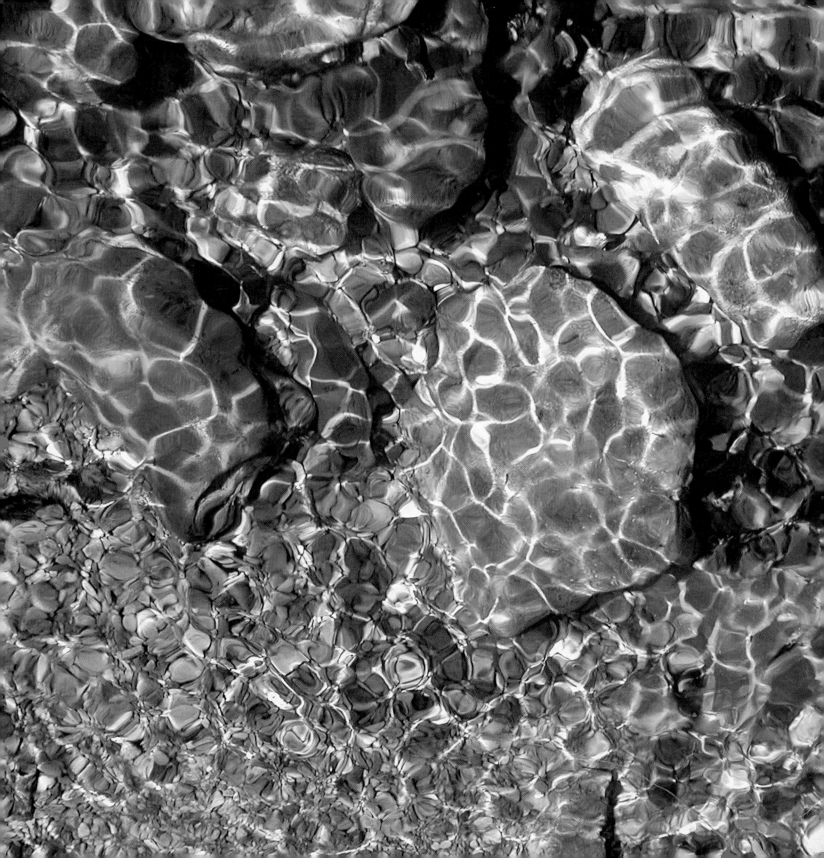

By hand, regular knitting with two yarns simultaneously and then separately is not impossible, but it is nonetheless quite tricky. Another method that can be used is 'Swiss darning' embroidery (see photos on pages 88 and 89).

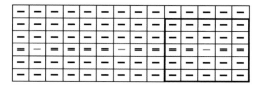

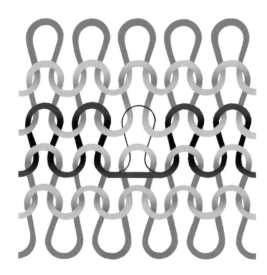

Fishnet or thread lace jacquard – face

Reverse

Using the intarsia method, it is possible to design motifs with different coloured areas, from wide to very narrow (i.e. down to one wale of knit loops), without changing the thickness of the fabric. The weight of intarsia knitwear is considerably reduced, since it is the same as single jersey; it is supple and gives the appearance of having been hand-knitted. This technique is becoming increasingly more cost-effective.

In the near future, it is likely to take up a dominant position and be used for three-dimensional creations, as not only can the number of colours in the same course be very large, the knit can also include very different stitch structures (see the following sections) as well as areas of float jacquard. Some machines have the facility to knit fishnet jacquards in intarsia. The knit is 'embroidered' (or 'partially plated') and takes on the appearance of a devoré textile (see treatments in chapter 1).

Until recently, the most frequently used intarsia designs were constructed with diagonals to form diamond shapes, such as the Argyle motif that is popular in menswear collections for sweaters and socks. Intarsia has also been frequently used for childrenswear to create figurative scenes including cartoon characters, and for womenswear, to make geometric or abstract compositions in a profusion of stunning fibres.

On domestic machines, this structure is achieved manually, without programming, by pressing the 'slip' keys and the 'intarsia' button, or by using a specially designed carriage. The needles must all be in position C. Then, starting from the main carriage side, simply lay the yarns in the needle hooks, holding the yarns while allowing them to slide, and pass the carriage to knit. This operation is then repeated for each course, crossing the yarns at each change of colour so as to avoid holes. To enhance this fabric with structures other than jersey, use hand-tooling techniques. In some cases, it is faster and easier to resort to hand-knitting intarsia.

Hand-knitting of intarsia does not present any particular problems, other than the risk of the different little balls of yarn becoming entangled.

Whether on a machine or by hand, in float jacquard or intarsia, when a colour is used in very small amounts, it is often better not to knit it but to add it after knitting by embroidering using the technique of 'Swiss darning' (see photos on pages 88 and 89).

Pages 88–89 (overleaf, bottom):
Swiss-darning embroidery
a – Put the needle in at the foot of a stitch.
b – Cover the side of this stitch and pass the needle behind the stitch in the row above.
c – Cover the second side of the stitch and put the needle again into the same stitch.
d, e – To embroider a row of stitches, sew into the foot of the stitch to the right or left and repeat as before.
f, g – To embroider a wale of stitches, sew into the foot of the stitch immediately above.
h – To embroider stitches at a distance from each other, sew into the foot of any stitch, making a float on the reverse.

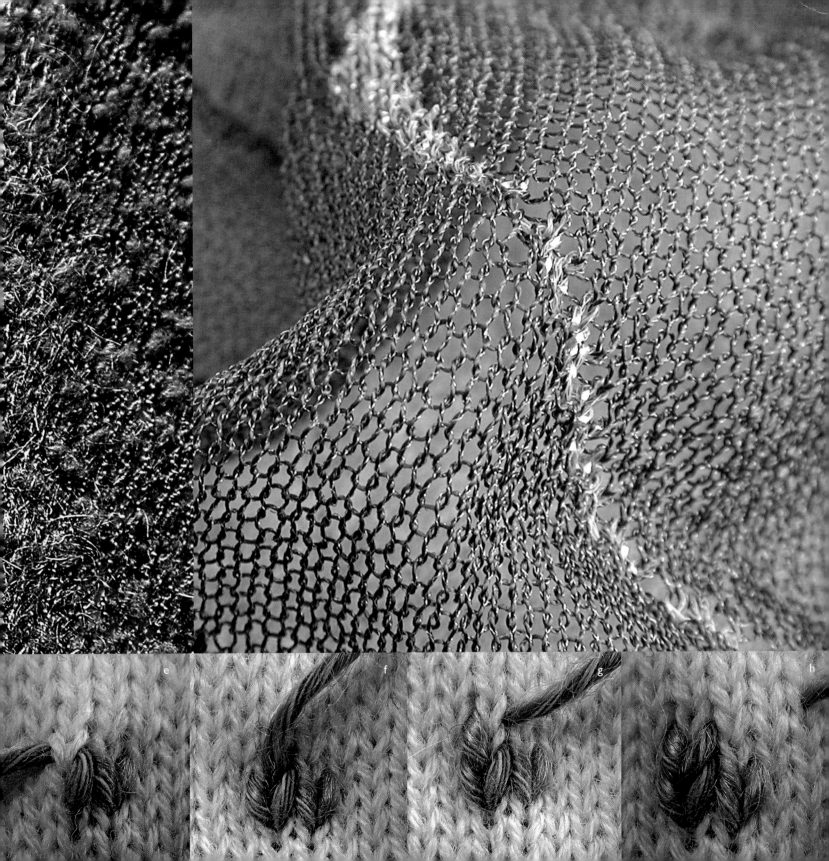

Float jersey jacquards:
Page 76 – Two-colour jacquard.
Page 77
1, 2 – Jacquard face and reverse.
4 – Jacquard with two yarns of very different fibre
and count.
5, 7, 8 – Jacquard knitted with a shrinkable yarn.
3 – Jacquard knit side with needles out.
6 – Jacquard purl side, hand embroidered.

Fishnet or thread lace jacquard:
9, 10, 11, 12, 13, 14 – see captions on page 80.

Intarsia jersey:
15, 16, 17 – Reverse jersey. The ends of the yarn can be
seen before and after knitting.
18 – Intarsia made with different yarns and materials,
reverse jersey.
19 – Intarsia with holes deliberately made between the
different coloured areas: the yarns are not crossed.
Page 85 – The same technique, but all the yarns are
identical.
Page 87 – Intarsia made with a destructible yarn which
vanishes with water or heat, felted to avoid the
stitches running.

Embroidered jacquard:
Pages 88 (20), 89 (21) and 90 (22) – Intarsia made with
partial plating or embroidery stitches. In sample 20, the
russet and green yarns are knitted in their own fields
and the blue yarn knits across the whole width.
Page 90 (23, 24) – The same process as for the
previous samples but using a yarn that contains Lycra.

5 'Suspended' stitches

Held stitches and floats

These structured knits – also called 'missed' or 'slipped' stitches – are characterized by courses containing both plain knitted stitches and one or more elongated stitches corresponding to needles that are not used to knit. During one or more consecutive courses these needle loops are temporarily held and elongate in length on the knit face, and on the reverse, the yarn connecting the needles that have knitted floats across between them, concealing the elongated stitches. The held loops give the impression of holes, and the floats create a range of textured effects, depending on their arrangement, the type of yarn and the tension setting. The knitting becomes finer and somewhat tighter in the direction of the courses, slightly losing the elastic qualities normally found in jersey, and giving the fabric physical characteristics closer to those found in weaving. Generally, the side on which the floats appear is used as the right side, but the fabrics are reversible. For a normal knitted fabric, it is best to avoid floats that are too long, as they are at risk of snagging. Textural relief patterns can be created on the knit side by building up floats over a number of adjacent needles over several courses. These relief or cloqué effects can be accentuated if the held loops are made from elastomeric yarn.

Industrially, these structures are often made in fine gauge. Sometimes the float side may also be brushed to obtain a fleecy surface (see chapter 17).

On domestic machines, fabrics containing held loops are made by programming a design using the 'slip' buttons on the carriage – the needles that are not selected do not knit.

Jacquards with three or four colours to a course are made using the same settings. Each colour is knitted separately for two traverses of the carriage (if using an automatic colour changer). For a four-colour jacquard, the carriage will make eight traverses to produce two knitted courses.

Knitting stripes with a specially designed programme enables colour jacquards to be produced in which the number of courses varies according to the number of colours used, causing subtle wavy effects both vertically and horizontally.

In hand-knitting, 'held' stitches are simply made by slipping stitches from one needle to the other, as they come up, without knitting or purling, for one or more rows.

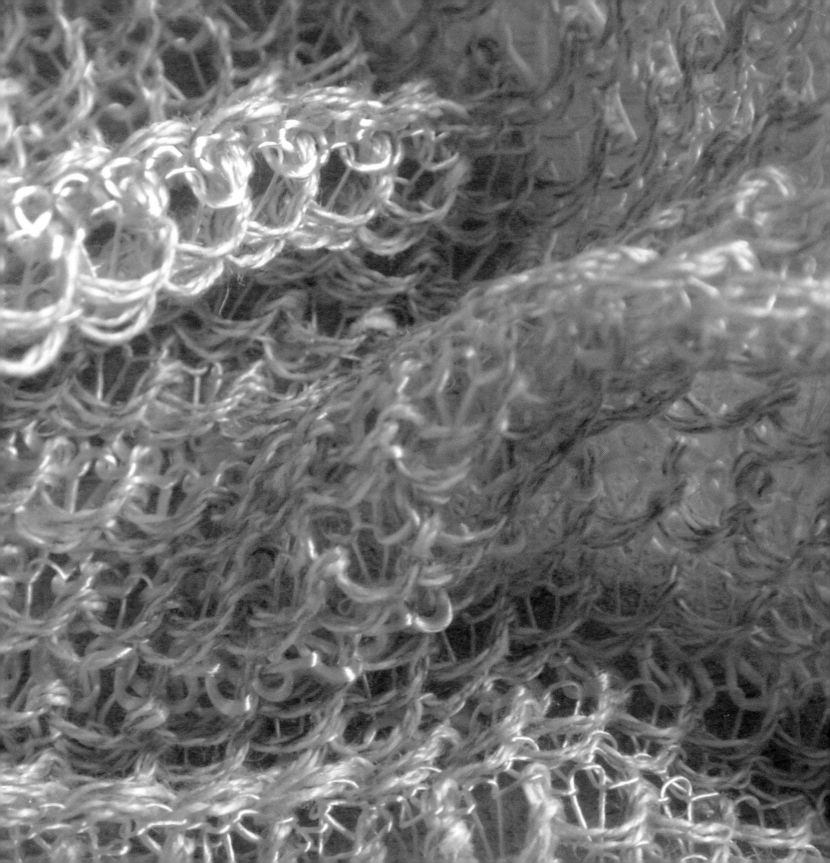

Slip-stitch knit side, technical face (wrong side)

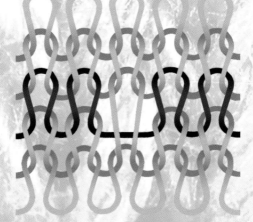

Purl side, technical reverse (generally right side)

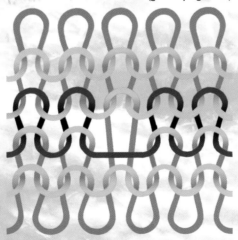

1
2
3

In principle, the floats appear on the reverse (purl) side but it is possible for them all to appear on the face (knit) side. In the latter case, on industrial machines, a completely different process is used to do this (see chapter 13) but in hand-knitting, all that is required is to take the yarn sometimes to the knit side and sometimes to the purl side of stocking stitch. The main difficulty lies in controlling the stitch length, as there is a tendency for the tension to be too tight. To avoid this problem, first knit as normal the stitches that are to be held, then on one or more following rows, unravel these stitches for one or more rows.

Partial knitting (*fléchage*)

Partial knitting (or *fléchage*) enables individual groups of needles to be held without knitting to obtain shaped or 'fully-fashioned' knitting. For example, on older industrial machines, shoulders used to be knitted one at a time. Now machines with independent yarn guides and several feeders can knit them simultaneously.

This facility allows work to be created in three dimensions, but also in any direction; this can be seen, for example, in the heel of a sock. Modern flat-bed machines are able to make highly sophisticated three-dimensional items.

The use of the partial knitting method also enables spectacular structures to be created with stitches at any angle, and which can also be highly textural. In this case, some needles are inactive for many courses, while others knit several courses of jersey, colour jacquard, float stitches, or tucks. (For fabrics made using the lace carriage, a suitable casting-on thread is used to hold the stitches of the inactive needles back in position A during the partial knitting.)

In industry, these effects are obtained on machines equipped with presser-foot systems, most frequently in fine gauge.

Most domestic machines have a partial knitting setting that will be explained in the section of the manual dealing with the making of garments. More unusual structures are not normally mentioned, but the settings are the same. Some needles must be held 'out of action' while the others knit, with or without a needle selection, according to the structure being used. If there is no special setting for partial knitting, it is, nevertheless, still possible to manually knit very long stitches using a waste yarn, then push these needles (with their stitches) completely back out of action, where they remain until required. Then all that is needed is to pull on one end of the waste yarn to bring the needles back into working position and unravel the waste yarn.

In hand-knitting, the stitches for partial knitting are held on a safety pin or by a specially designed accessory. Fancy stitches can be made using double-pointed needles, enabling a section of the work to be knitted from the right side and wrong side alternately. Fabrics made in this way can be striking and unusual, but are generally very time-consuming.

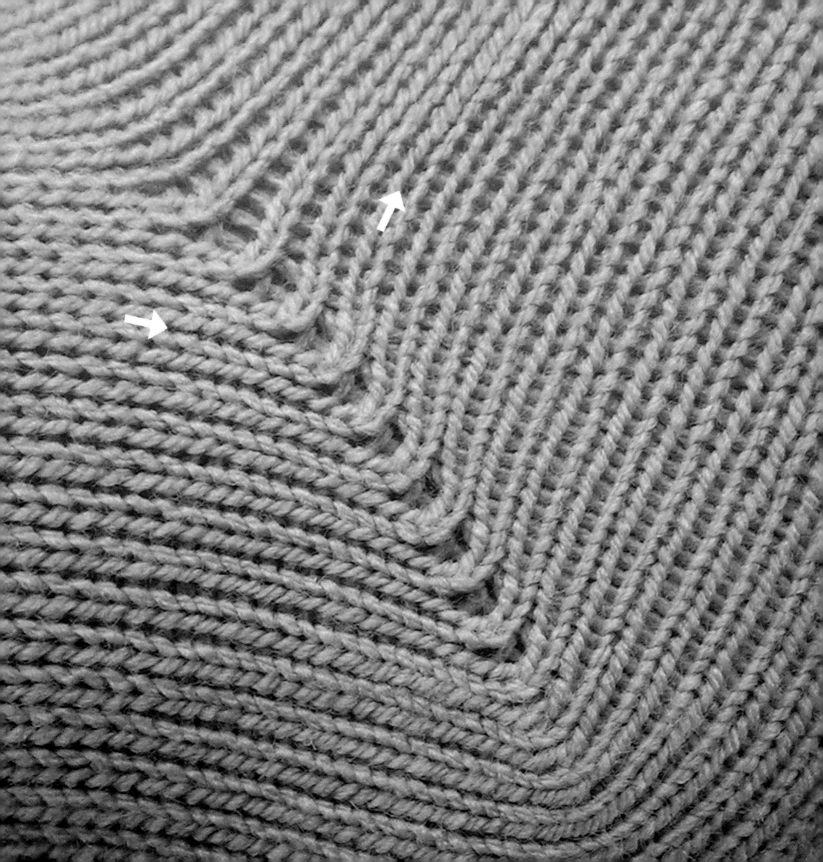

18

19

20

Pages 95 and 98–99 (1, 2, 3, 4) – Small designs containing held or slipped stitches, and consequently floats, reverse jersey (purl) side.

Pages 98–99 – Knitting with contrast stripes and slip stitches – therefore colour jacquard.
5, 6, 7 – The wales comprise a number of different courses: if the designs are fairly large, undulating effects sometimes appear in the alignment of stitches on the knit side.
8 – Supplementary courses are knitted in intarsia.

Partial knitting or *fléchage*:
Pages 103 (sock heel) and 104 (9, 10) – Partial knitting enables the constraints of knitting in just one direction to be conquered, including knitting in the vertical direction and, by extension, in any direction.
Page 104
11, 12 – The technique of 'split stitch' avoids holes appearing in the fabric at the point where the number of courses changes on the knit side.
13, 14, 17 – Knitting a large number of courses in small areas creates either three-dimensional effects or holes.
15, 16 – Multiple sock heels, plain and striped. Partial knitting on some needles and over several courses, repeated regularly over the entire course.

Variations of partial knitting:
Page 106 – Spiral knitting.
Page 107
18 – Structure similar to numbers 13 and 14 and knitted Lycra with needles out.
19 – The same process, made in an irregular manner.
20 – Spiral, stripes and chains: partial knitting on individual needles.
Page 108 (21, 22, 23) – Jersey jacquard with floats.

6 Tuck stitch fabrics

These are knits that comprise a mix of plain stitches and tuck stitches. A tuck is formed when the yarn is collected by a needle without knitting it as the carriage is traversed. Tuck stitches affect the texture of the fabric in the following ways:

- if the needle which receives the loop was previously empty, a new wale is created with a gap at the base.
- if the needle already has a stitch, this stitch and the tuck loop are knitted together. Consequently, the stitch is larger but flatter; the fabric thickens; the legs of the tuck loop stand out and create diagonal relief effects on the purl side of the fabric. According to the positioning and frequency of the tucks, and depending on the tension settings, the courses and wales appear wavy, particularly on the knit side of the fabric.
- if several tucks accumulate on the same needle over several courses, the relief effect is accentuated and becomes a knop. The knitting that has continued around the knop gathers and puckers up.

The textured tuck fabrics most frequently found have a cellular appearance on the purl side of the fabric, and a piqué effect of small markings on the knit side, or a 'fishnet' appearance when knitted on half-gauge, or raised knop effects on the knit side when several tucks have been made on certain needles. A crepe surface effect is obtained when tucks are arranged randomly. Tuck stitch effects can also be accentuated by plating. In this case, the legs of the tucks appear in a contrast colour or fibre on the purl side of the jersey base. Tucked fabrics are usually flexible with a bubbly surface.

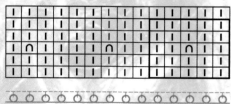

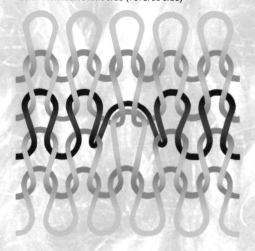

Tuck stitch fabric knit side (reverse side)

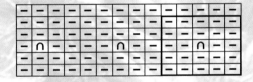

Purl side (usually the face or right side)

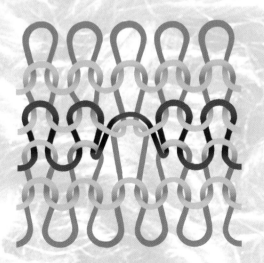

Coloured tuck jacquards without floats can be knitted by using tuck stitches in a specially designed pattern programme, in combination with colour stripes. Slight wavy effects are created along both the courses and the wales.

On domestic machines, tuck stitch fabrics can be obtained using a programmed design and a mechanical setting of the carriage. On single-bed machines, without exception, tuck stitches can never be adjacent in the same course. However, they can be accumulated over several consecutive courses. It is important to carefully check the positioning of the tucks during the preparation of a design.

In order to mix together different structures with tuck stitches, it can sometimes be interesting to create them manually. With a hand tool, pick up a loop from the previous course (or earlier), and let the stitch drop down to the tool. Then slip the stitch and the floats just obtained onto the needle that corresponds to that wale, to be knitted in the next course.

The same setting which holds needles in position D (for partial knitting) also enables tuck stitches to be made. All that is required is to push individual needles to position D at random across the width of the knitting (in this technique, some needles can be adjacent). When the carriage knits, a float is created over these needles, then when the 'partial knitting' setting is cancelled, they return to knitting, forming tucks at the same time.

In hand-knitting, tuck stitches can be made by knitting into the stitch below the next loop on the needle, or by knitting into a stitch two or three rows below to create double or triple tuck stitches. Another method is to make a 'yarn over' before or after slipping a stitch, then knitting the slipped stitch and the yarn over loop together in the following row. For a triple tuck, proceed in the same way for the first row, then in the second row pass the same slipped stitch and yarn over onto the other needle without knitting, then make another yarn over. On the third row knit the two yarn overs together with the slipped stitch.

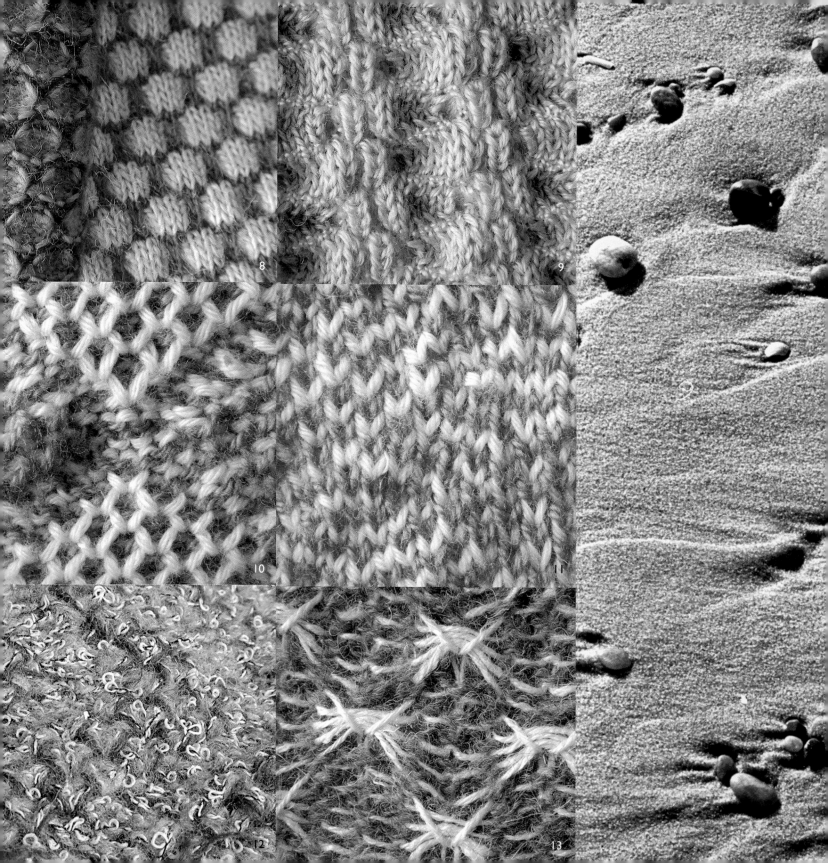

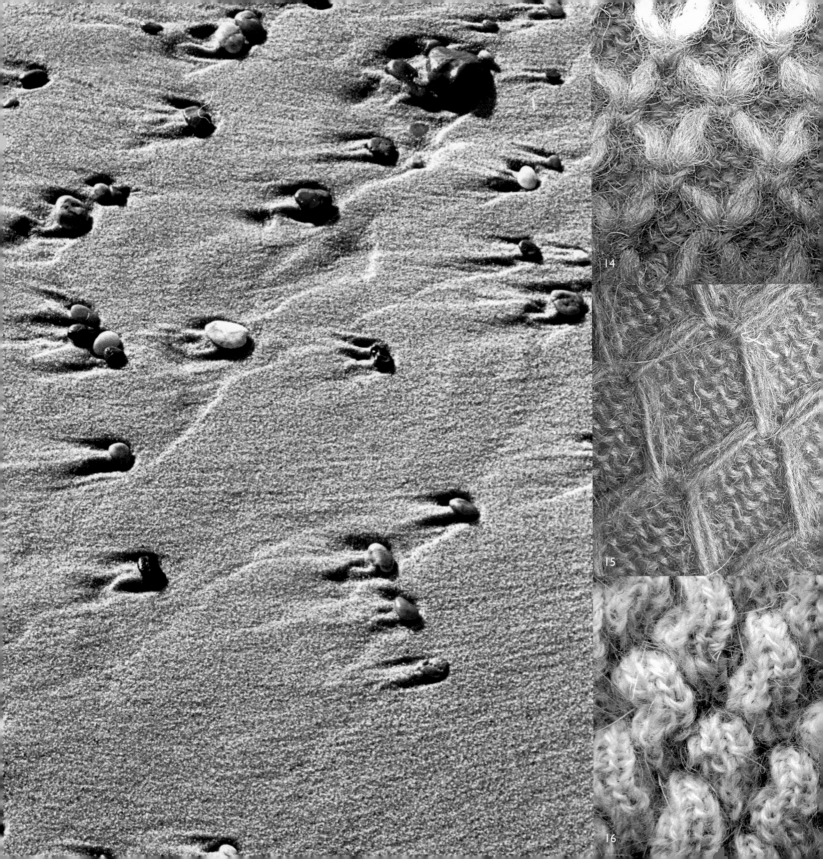

14

15

16

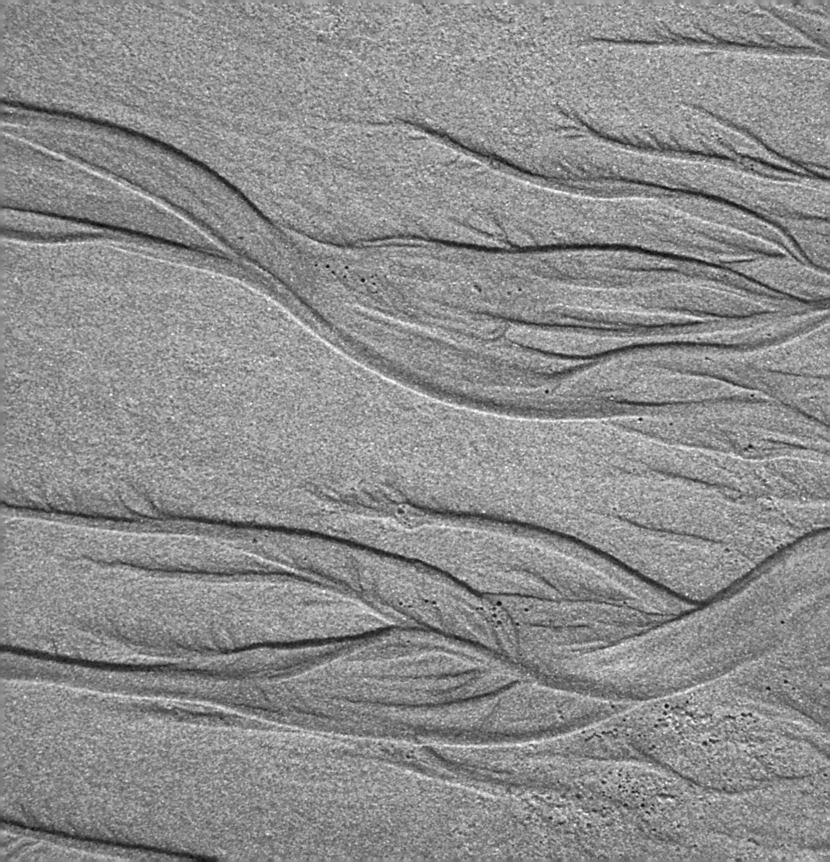

Inlay or weaving

This particular technique allows the insertion into a knitted fabric of a second yarn, which may be extremely thick or may have an unusual fancy structure. This yarn is not knitted, but lays on the surface of the technical back (purl or reverse jersey side) of the fabric, held in place by the feet of the knitted loops. These fabrics have similar characteristics to woven textiles. The knitting loses its normal elasticity, unless of course either the knitting or the inlay yarn is made from elastomeric yarn.

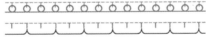

Inlay knit side (reverse)

Inlay purl side (face or right side)

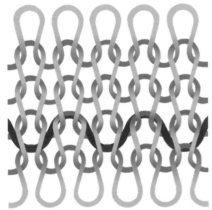

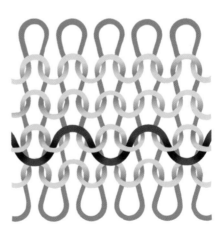

17

20

Inlay can be used all over, interrupted by bands of plain jersey or other stitches, or used partially across the width of a panel. This process is used in industry, notably to obtain fleecy fabrics. After knitting, a fluffy surface is created by brushing the inlay yarn, which is sometimes partially sheared, in order to create relief effects in the fleece.

In some single-bed jacquards, extra long floats can be incorporated into the reverse of the fabric in the same manner as inlay. Certain pleat effects can be made with tuck stitches: an elastane yarn is passed across the back of the knitting, which is picked up at intervals onto a needle, creating a tuck. After knitting, steaming contracts the elastane and the fabric puckers. The nature of the three-dimensional effect created depends on the positioning of the tucks.

On domestic machines inlaid or woven fabrics are made using a programme. The brushes are lowered in order to press the fancy inlay yarn close to the needles. The inlay yarn is then placed manually into the appropriate yarn guide. When interspersing woven knitting with bands of jersey or jacquard, the weaving yarn can be left aside at the selvedge. However, if weaving across part of the course only (partial knitting), the cone of fancy yarn must be placed on the floor. Needles are then selected manually and the inlay yarn is laid over the selected needles only. Then, guiding the yarn by hand while allowing it to run freely, the carriage knits with the main yarn. By this method it is also possible to create fabrics using several different inlay yarns in the same course (similar to the intarsia technique).

To obtain single jersey jacquards with woven-in floats, the longer floats are picked up onto a nearby needle with a latch tool, before the course is knitted.

In hand-knitting, inlay is obtained by knitting with two yarns together, in a fairly delicate operation. One yarn is used for the main knitting and the other is guided by hand, above and below the stitches according to the desired design. Care must be taken not to pull the weaving yarn too tight, as the width of the knitting will be reduced, resulting in a bumpy surface. Weaving can also be done once the knitting is finished, by working a yarn in and out of the feet of the stitches with an embroidery needle.

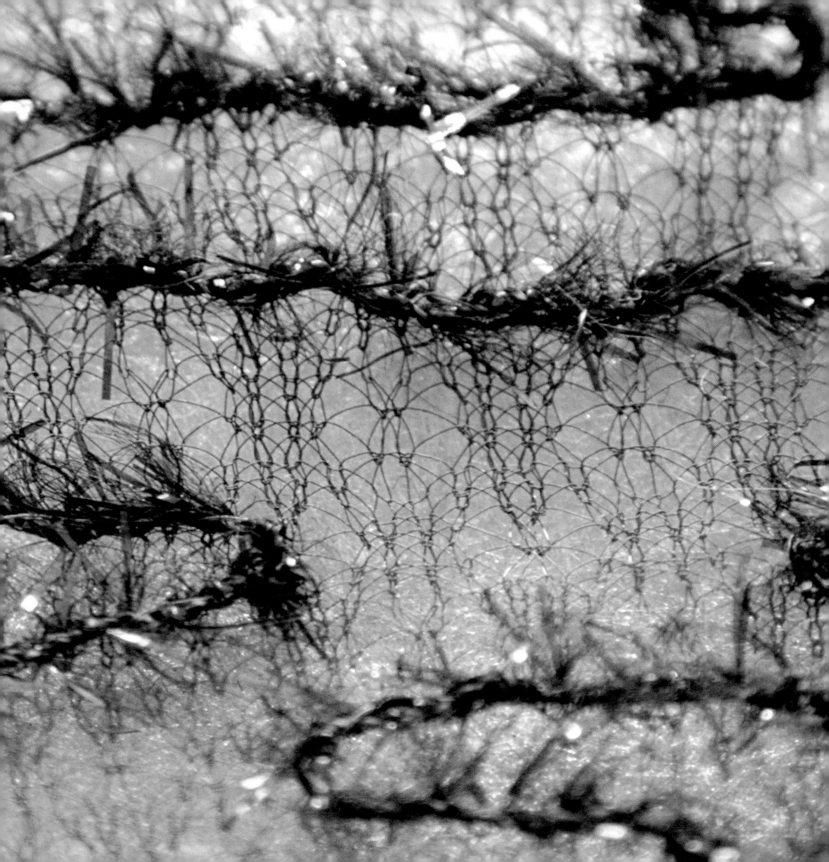

Page 115
1 – Design created from a small cellular motif made with tucks arranged alternately in staggered rows, purl side.
3 – Same design, knit side: piqué appearance.
2, 4, 6 – Knopped texture made by the accumulation of tucks over several courses, purl side and knit side.
5 – Openwork tuck stitch made with missing needles.
7 – Needle-out fabric with tucking.
Page 116 – Unevenly spaced tucks giving a crepe effect.

Page 118 – Tuck jacquards
8, 9 – Relief patterned samples knitted with stripes for a jacquard effect in several colours without floats: the wales and courses undulate.
10, 11 – A similar process to the above, face and reverse.
12 – Plating, purl side.
13 – Jacquard with accumulation of four tucks on each needle, repeated alternately.

Page 119 – Giant tucks
14 – With contrast stripes.
15 – Self-coloured.
16 – Knitted with a shrinkable yarn: the three-dimensional texture is accentuated.

Page 121 – Pleats and waves
At top (face and reverse) and below – samples created by making the tucks with an elastic yarn.

Inlay or weaving made with a fancy yarn tucking on the surface, this yarn has a much heavier count than the yarn that knits: it runs across the whole width of the piece without being knitted.

Page 124
17, 18 – Purl side.
19 – Knit side.
20, 21 – Jersey jacquard, knit side and purl side: on the knit side, the legs of the stitches show through between the wales; on the purl side, the floats – which have to be very long for this pattern – have been picked up onto every alternate needle with a hand tool, then knitted the following course.

Page 128 – Fancy yarn embroidered onto a ground of transparent openwork tuck fabric.

7 Purl or links-links fabrics

These are patterned knits in which the wales and courses comprise both knit and purl loops, and which do not have a 'wrong' side. If the design appears in knit stitches on a purl ground from one side, then from the other it appears as purl stitches on a knit ground. Garter stitch (which should not be confused with the reverse of jersey fabric), like moss stitch, and some stripes and checks, looks the same on both sides of the knitting. These fabrics are supple, light and some are very stretchy.

In the industry, double-bed machines are used to create purl fabrics. The process does not have any technical constraints and the sampling possibilities are unlimited. Basic structures in small repeats provide many surface textures, but compositions can also be geometric, abstract or figurative, and can extend across the entire width of the needlebed. However, all patterns are not of equal interest, but it is advisable to take care in the charting of designs as some combinations of knit and purl can create surprising effects that are difficult to imagine from the charting alone.

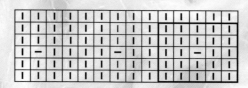

One purl stitch on a knit stitch ground

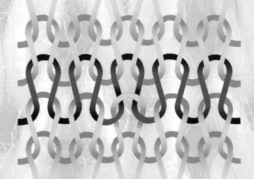

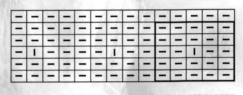

One knit stitch on a purl stitch ground

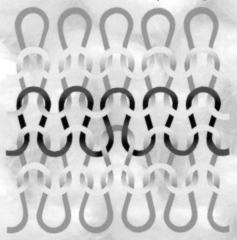

Practice and observation confirms that jersey fabric is not flat. It rolls towards the purl (reverse) side in the direction of the wales, and towards the knit (face) side in the direction of the courses. This characteristic also affects each individual stitch, which curls in the same manner, causing interesting physical effects: across the width, the knit loops appear in relief, while along the length they are sunken (see examples on the following pages). These curling effects also change the proportions of the fabric. For the same number of stitches and courses made in horizontal bands (like garter stitch) purl fabrics are wider and thicker. In the case of vertical bands (ribs), the opposite is true. Some particular combinations of stitches therefore create curved movements in the courses and wales. To maintain these effects in certain purl fabrics, it is best to press them only lightly.

In industry, this type of knitting can easily be plated. Purl fabrics can also be combined with slipped stitches, colour jacquards and tuck stitches, cabled stitches and openwork knitted fabrics.

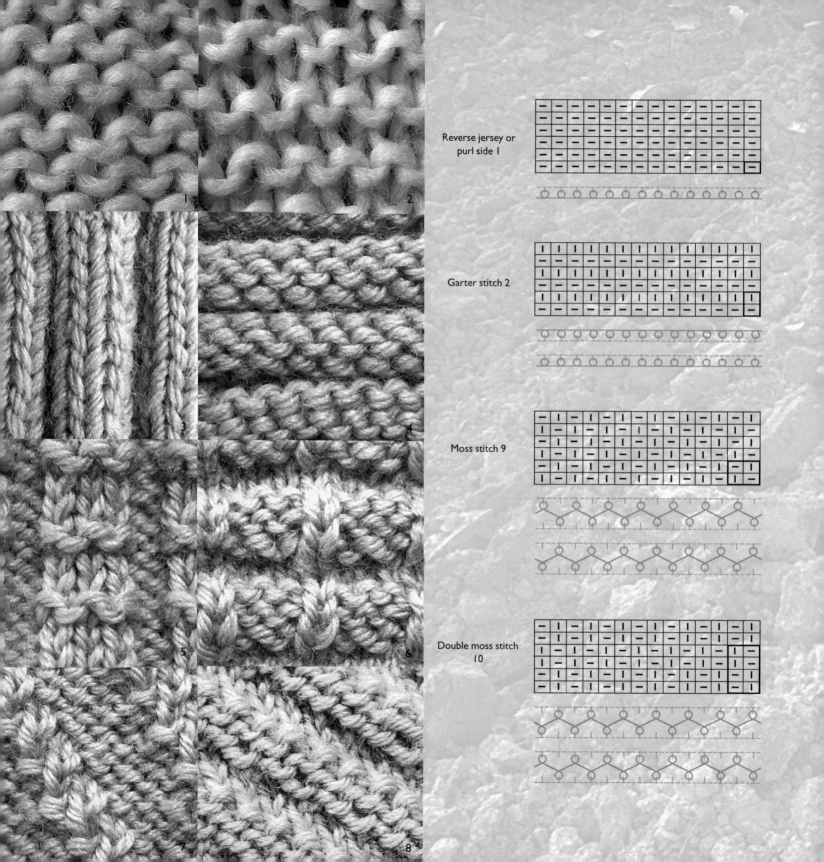

Reverse jersey or
purl side 1

Garter stitch 2

Moss stitch 9

Double moss stitch
10

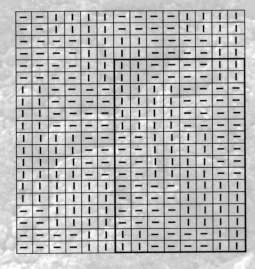

Chequerboard or basket weave check 11

Step or wave pattern 13

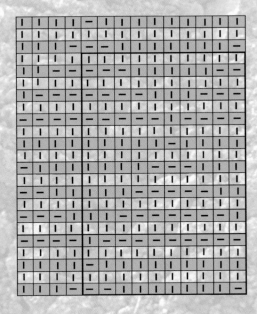

14

9

10

11

12

13

14

15

16

17

18

19

23   24   25

Some domestic machines have an electronic attachment (garter carriage) which knits purl stitches on the back needlebed, following a pre-programmed design. If the machine has two needlebeds, it is possible to reverse the stitches manually with a hand tool (i.e. to transfer them to the opposite needlebed) then to knit with the carriage and repeat according to the design. If the design involves a high number of transfers, in the end it may be preferable to use hand-knitting.

By hand, garter stitch is obtained in a straight piece of knitting by repeating the same stitch, i.e. knitting or purling, indefinitely. For other structures that combine knit and purl stitches in the same course, the yarn must be moved between (and not below!) the needles: the yarn must be at the back of the knitting for a knit stitch, and in front for a purl stitch. To accomplish the knitting of a complex structure or a design of medium to large size, it is best to prepare the design on graph paper.

8 Tubular knitting

Tubular knits

These are fabrics that have a cylindrical shape. They may have different diameters depending on the diameter of the machine, and the courses of stitches are built up in a spiral formation. Lengths of tubular fabric are usually presented folded flat or rolled lengthwise.

They are made on circular knitting machines with one or two needlebeds, and on flat double-bed machines, usually in medium, fine or extra fine gauge. The textiles produced are either technical products destined for a specific end use, or used for the making up of cut and sewn clothing. The smallest tubular knit is the cord, usually consisting of four needles. Some yarns are made using this technique: some of them are set during the knitting process; others are pressed, as in some braids and shoe laces.

Structural variations are possible in tubular knitting, depending on the particular machine used: some make only plain and striped jersey, others can do any type of stitch, but in general, most machines specialize in particular groups of knitted fabrics, such as pile fabric machines, sock machines, and so on. Gloves, which are integrally knitted tubular articles, are made on specialist flat machines. Using the same principle – tubular knitted fabric made with partial knitting – it is possible to imagine any type of three-dimensional volume, although not all are practical to make. The latest flat-bed knitting machines with two or four needlebeds create tubular knitwear with ribbed and cabled patterning, but most importantly they enable the diameter of the pieces to be changed in order to fit the shape of the body (in a dress for example).

Fine gauge jersey textiles can undergo various finishing treatments, which may change their appearance completely (see chapter 1).

Tubular fabrics can also be produced on double-bed domestic machines in a similar way; that is, by knitting on only one needlebed at a time in each direction, for example, one traverse on the back bed only, and the return traverse on the front bed only, a sequence that is repeated indefinitely. The number of needles knitting can vary anywhere between 2 and 400. Double the width of fabric can be obtained by semi-circular knitting: knit first on one bed, then on the other, then on the second one again, then on the first one and so on, repeated throughout.

On domestic machines, tubular or semi-circular knitting can be created in jersey, striped jersey, half-gauge jersey or openwork jersey with various needles out of action. Fabrics with tucks, slipped stitches, or colour jacquards can be made if the patterns are charted on a graph with multiples of two stitches by two rows, as domestic machines are only programmable on the back bed. On the front bed, there is a mechanical setting that enables every other needle to be selected; these then alternate with every course. In practice, it is impossible to create tubular fabrics with purl stitch patterning, or with ribs on existing domestic machines. To achieve a tubular form, the two edges of a flat panel can be sewn together with an embroidery needle, using Swiss darning.

In contrast, in hand-knitting, any circular fabric can be made using three of four double-pointed needles to hold the stitches and one to knit with: there may be four or five needles used in turn. A special circular needle can also be used, consisting of a flexible plastic section with a knitting needle at each end.

Knitted cords used to be made on a wooden cotton reel with nails in the top and commercially made toys are still available, based on the same principle. There also exists a small plastic apparatus that works with a handle and greatly speeds up the output.

Double-face fabrics

These are double-bed fabrics, generally made in fairly fine gauges. They consist of two jersey fabrics (with knit side on the outside) connected together by loops of the yarn. There are several types of double-faced knitted textiles:

- each face of the fabric is identical: this is a tubular knit of which the two sides are held together by loops made on certain needles of the opposite needlebed. The linkages between the two faces can be regularly distributed amongst the wales and courses with any chosen interval, or even distributed according to a pattern defined by a jacquard selection.
- one of the faces is knitted with a shrinkable yarn – this produces a blister fabric with a depth of relief patterning that depends on the count of the yarn and the tension settings used on the side with the shrinking yarn. The quantity and distribution of the linkages naturally also affects the appearance of these fabrics.

To accentuate the textural relief effects, it is also possible to knit a number of extra courses on one side. These effects can be exaggerated on flat-bed machines by racking the needlebeds (see chapter 10). By missing out some wales on the reverse (and/or the right side), it is possible to lighten the knitted fabric. To create pronounced relief effects, industrial machines must be equipped with a presser foot or sinkers to hold down the knitting.

On domestic machines, to obtain linking stitches that will hold the two fabrics together, either manually pull out several needles to position D on the needlebed, where they will be held, or use a programme on the back needlebed. But pay attention: the needles must never be opposite each other when working with both needlebeds together; the beds must be racked to half-pitch. For structures with extreme blister effects, it is necessary to frequently reposition the weights, and to also bring needles out manually to position D on the side that is knitting, before each pass of the carriage.

To hand-knit double-faced fabrics, cast on double the stitches, then (*) knit 1, yarn forward, slip 1, yarn back (*) and repeat from (*) to (*). To hold the two surfaces together: work the knit stitches together with the foot of the following stitch. This is an interesting technique that can be used as a point of departure for experiments with more complex samples. However, in the majority of basic double-face fabrics, it may often be preferable to knit the two fabrics separately and to discreetly join them together by sewing with a transparent nylon yarn.

1

2

3

4

5

6

Page 147 – Gloves in plain jersey, right side/wrong side.
Page 148 – Metallic scourer.
Pages 150 and 151 (1, 2) – Double-face fabric knitted
with two different yarns.
Page 151
3 – Same process: one of the faces has been printed.
4, 5 – Double face with float stitch, face/reverse.
6 – One face plain and one face striped.
Page 152
7, 8 – Pocket fabric: the pattern is created by the
positioning of the linking stitches.
9 – Giant float fabric: the floats are cut to form fringes.
10 – Puckered knit made using Lycra in one face.
11 – Shirred effect created by knitting a different
number of courses on each face.
12 – Knitting with three layers at the same time.

9 Ribbed fabrics

By knitting simultaneously on two needlebeds, but not separately as in double-faced fabrics, ribbed fabrics are obtained.

These are fabrics structured in longitudinal lines. Needles are selected on each needlebed in staggered formation. Ribs therefore consist of alternating small or large bands of knit jersey and purl jersey. They also often contain tuck stitches or slipped stitches. In contrast to jersey, rib fabrics do not roll (unless of course made of very wide ribs). In industry, fine ribbed fabrics are made on both flat-bed machines and double jersey circular machines with two needlebeds.

Take care: needles that are in action must never be opposite each other, since the knitting of each course takes place simultaneously on both beds. Therefore the beds may need to be re-positioned at half pitch according to the particular structure being created.

Basic ribs

Basic one by one and full needle ribs, two by two, or special broad ribs such as six by three (Derby rib) or two by ten, or fancy ribs with irregular rhythms, will vary in their three-dimensional effects and stretch properties depending on the actual width of the ribs, which tend to roll both to the inside and the outside. The fabric is wavy and varies in thickness. Richelieu (or Milano) ribs are arrangements of one by one ribs and jersey: on one needlebed all the needles are in action, and on the other, some needles are out of action.

In fine ribbing, the rolling effect is hardly noticeable along the length of the fabric. The knitting remains flat, compact and stable: only the knit stitches are visible. In fabrics containing broader ribs, the purl stitches are visible, sunk between the knit stitches which appear in relief. All rib fabrics are reversible: sometimes they are the same on both sides, sometimes they have a positive/negative appearance. Rib structures are also frequently used as finishings for collars and cuffs, to tighten the edges and prevent them from rolling. Ribs can also be plated or knitted in stripes.

On domestic machines, ribs can be made with the 'garter carriage' attachment together with a programme, or made more quickly using two needlebeds, with an appropriate needle selection knitting plain on each bed.

In hand-knitting, ribs are simply knitted or purled as the stitches present themselves. For example, a one by one rib is made by the method: yarn back, knit 1, yarn forward, purl 1, and repeat.

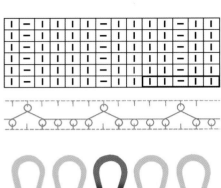

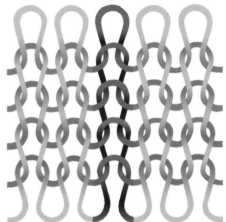

1 x 4 rib, face

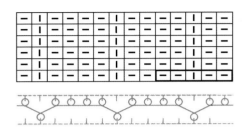

Reverse

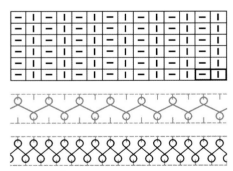

1 x 1 rib and full needle rib layouts

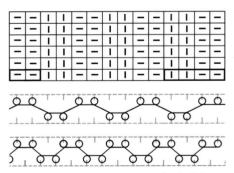

2 x 2 rib layouts

Tuck ribs

These ribbed fabrics combine knit and purl stitches with tuck stitches. The knit stitches become enlarged but more compressed together, concealing the purl stitches. These fabrics are very flexible, bulky, slightly heavier and very stretchy.

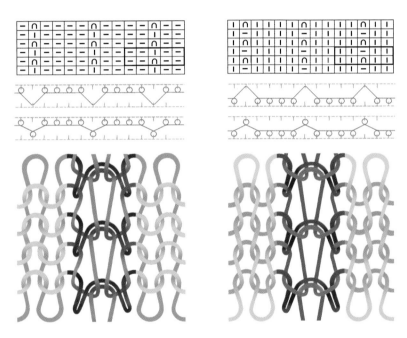

Rib with the tucks on the reverse of knit stitches

Reverse with tucks on the face of the purl stitches

    For the same number of stitches and courses of a basic rib, samples made with tuck stitches are much shorter and wider. This tendency can be exploited to change the width of a knitted fabric without changing the number of needles used (for frilled edgings or for fitting a garment from the waist to the bust). If the two types of rib are used alternately in the same piece, an undulating effect is produced along the length of the fabric.

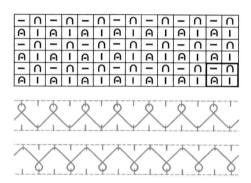

Here are two commonly used versions of tuck ribs:

• fisherman's rib or full cardigan rib has two identical faces. It is knitted in two steps: one course consists of plain knit stitches alternating with tuck stitches on the opposite needlebed; the second consists of the reverse – tuck stitches alternating with plain stitches on the opposite bed. The knit loops, supported on the legs of the tucks, are most prominent, with the purl stitches totally hidden. If during knitting, the yarn is changed every course, vertical two-colour ribs are obtained, but on both sides of the fabric in a positive/negative effect, as for beaded rib.

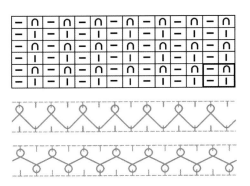

• beaded rib or half cardigan is made in two stages, one course of one by one rib, and one course consisting of a plain stitch alternating with a tuck stitch on the opposite bed. These two courses are repeated throughout the whole length of the fabric. The two sides are different: on the tuck side, the purl stitches and the sides of the tucks appear distinctly, forming small equilateral triangles on top of each other. On the other side, the purl stitches disappear beneath the legs of the knit stitches. The tucks (like held loops) allow courses to be suppressed on some wales, and consequently, by changing the yarn on every course, coloured jacquard can be obtained: on the tuck side showing vertical furrows in two colours, on the other side 'beaded' stripes that are slightly blurred.

The bulkiness of these ribs can be accentuated by doubling (or more) the tucks on the needles. They can also be plated, striped, or for jacquard-based fabrics, made with yarns which vary in count, fibre and texture.

On domestic machines, this type of rib is obtained with two needlebeds. For a beaded rib, the carriage settings are as follows: on the back bed, set to 'plain' [*] on the front bed, from right to left, set to 'plain', and from left to right set to 'tuck'[*] (or inversely from [*] to [*]) For fisherman's rib the carriage is set, for example, to 'tuck' from right to left and to 'plain' from left to right on the back bed, and on the front bed the settings are reversed.

Remember, in hand-knitting, tuck stitches are called double or triple stitches (see chapter 6).

Rib fabrics with slipped stitches

On the technical face, these fabrics comprise knit stitches which are slipped or held, on a ground of reverse jersey; on the technical back, the held loops do not show.

These ribs are made by holding needles on one needlebed only. They are knitted with stitches held for one or more courses. The held stitches, larger than the stitches of the background, appear prominently in relief. The knitting is fairly flat (depending on the width of jersey sections) and no longer stretchy.

The ground stitches can be knitted in stripes of two or more colours, creating a jacquard effect. The stitch loops can be held for one course (most often) or for several courses; they can also be highlighted by plating.

On domestic machines, these ribs can be obtained by positioning slipped stitches sometimes on the front bed, sometimes on the back bed, by setting the carriage to 'slip' on one traverse and to 'plain' on the return. On the opposite bed, all the needles knit in jersey. The tension setting on the bed with the held loops can be looser than on the bed that is knitting plain fabric.

In hand-knitting, the held stitches are slipped from one needle to the other, as they occur.

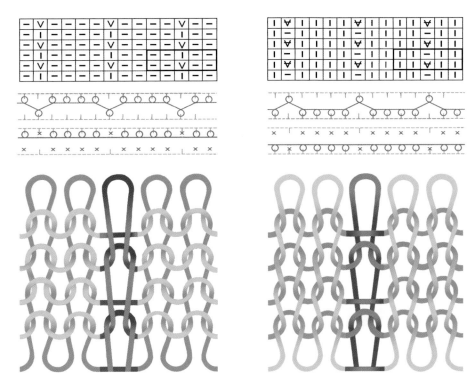

Rib with slipped or held stitches, face   Reverse

9   10   11

Pleats

In very fine fabrics, regular or random pleats can be obtained by heat pressing over blades (as in all textiles made primarily of polyester).

In fine gauge knitting, the combination of full needle rib,(or interlock, or rib jacquard: see the following chapters), in which the knitting stays flat, with single jersey, which curls widthways to the inside and to the outside, enables permanent pleated effects to be obtained simply by the arrangement of the needles selected.

The basic pleat formations are illustrated below: accordion pleats, flat or box pleats, and knife pleats folded either to the left or right.

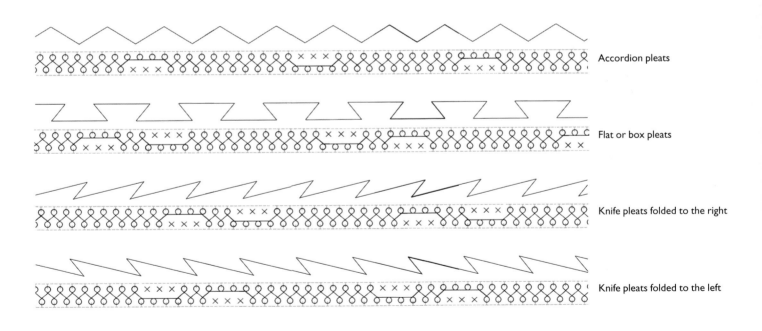

Accordion pleats

Flat or box pleats

Knife pleats folded to the right

Knife pleats folded to the left

12

13

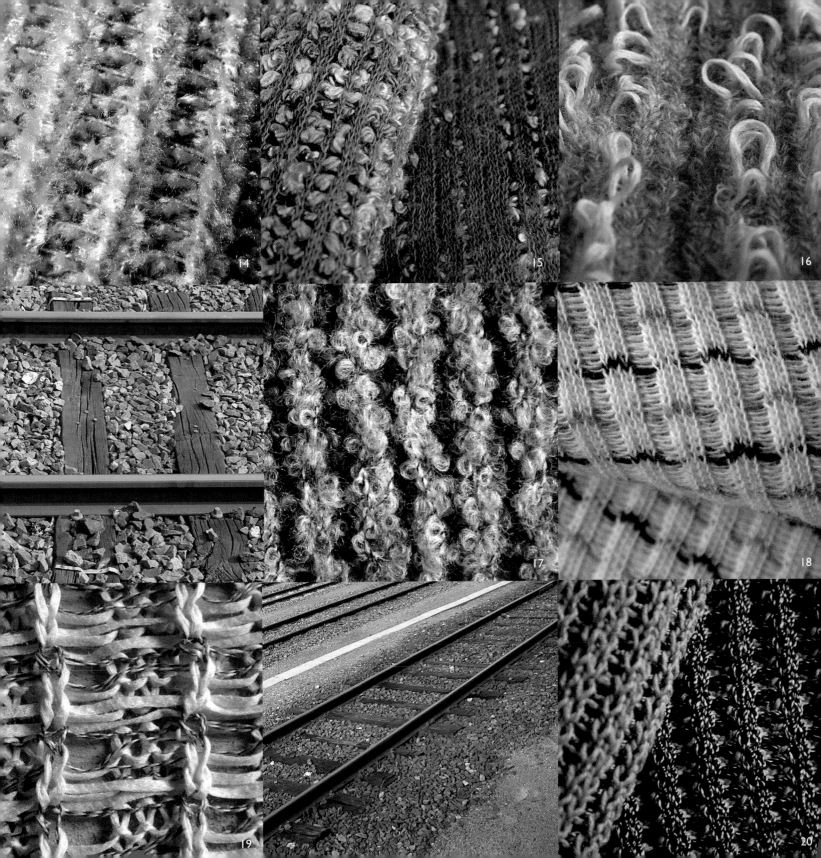

21

22

Fancy ribs

Derby ribs, tuck ribs, and slip-stitch ribs can be worked together in the same fabric. They can also be combined with structures introduced in other chapters.

It is possible to knit fancy ribs with floats, leaving needles out on one or both beds, either offset or opposite. They can incorporate transfers (openwork or cables), racking (see following chapter), plating, inlay, or many possible combinations.

On domestic machines and in hand-knitting, fancy ribs can be created by combining techniques from other chapters in the book, making use of graphs to avoid errors.

Page 158: Basic ribs
1 – 1 x 1 (full needle) rib looks the same on both face and reverse: the purl stitches disappear between the knit stitches.
2 – Half-gauged 1 x 1 rib.
3 – 2 x 2 rib with a jersey rolled or rouleau edging.
4 – Irregular fancy rib.

Page 160 – Frill made with fisherman's rib, tubular knitting and full needle rib; using the change in proportions of the ribs due to the different structures to adjust the width, the height and the thickness of the knitted fabric.

Page 162–163
5, 6 – Fisherman's rib or full cardigan, face and reverse, knitted in single course stripes using two yarns of slightly different count; the two colours appear as vertical stripes.
7, 8 – Beaded rib or half cardigan, face and reverse, made with the same yarns as the previous sample, also changing colour every course.

Page 165
9, 10 – Flat ribs.
11 – Broad rib with contrast stripes and held stitches.

Page 166: Vertical pleats.

Page 168
12 – Fancy rib with needles out and floats.
13 – Plated broad rib.

Page 169
14 – Inlaid rib using an elastic yarn.
15 – Inlaid rib, face and reverse.
16 – Inlaid rib made with a shrinkable yarn: the inlay yarn is trapped, forming loops in relief.
17 – 1 x 1 rib made with a bouclé yarn.
18, 19 – Fancy rib with open ladders, contrast stripes and slipped stitches.
20 – Fancy rib with tucks, knitted using two colours in stripes.
Page 170
21 – 1 x 1 rib, cast off stitches and partial knitting.
22, 23 – Ribs with partial knitting.

10 Racked stitches

Racking is a technique that means displacing one needlebed to the right or left in relation to the other one, by one or more notches or needle positions. The knit stitches of the front bed thus cross the purl stitches of the back bed, forming a pronounced diagonal stitch in relief. This technique does not use transfer stitches, and is consequently very fast and economical.

With an arrangement of needles similar to that used for ribbing, continuous racking without transferring creates waves or chevrons of variable width and height throughout the length of the knitting. For a long time, the extent of the racking was limited to a dozen notches. Recent industrial machines now enable a diagonal line to be maintained across the entire width of the fabric. In loosely knitted plain fabrics, racking one notch is hardly noticeable, but in fabrics with tuck stitches (such as fisherman's rib or beaded rib) or slipped stitches, the sloping effect is strongly accentuated. In openwork fabrics, racking has the effect of lightening the knitting and affects its depth and transparency.

Knitted fabrics containing both tuck stitches and racking can, depending on the needle arrangement, produce extremely striking effects: for example, structures that contain both racked and straight wales, or which have a three-dimensional 'egg-box' structure. The selvedges and borders of the knitting can be shaped with chevrons, which can also be used as a finish, or as a braid for trimmings.

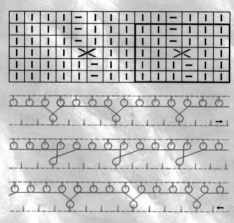

Racked knitting, right side

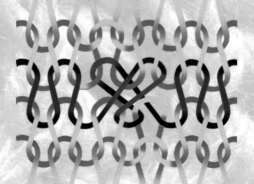

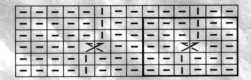

Reverse

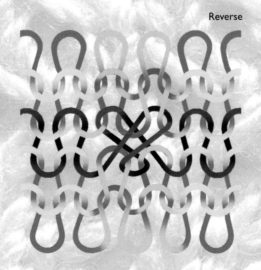

Racking can also be used in double-face fabrics, particularly in blister fabrics. In these, the stitches are knitted in tubular jersey and the two surfaces joined in certain places, after racking the beds, by making tuck or plain stitches on the opposite needlebed.

Racking is also used for casting on in ribbing, notably 'two by two' or 'three by three' ribs, without the need to transfer stitches.

On domestic machines, racking is done by turning a handle. Particular attention must be paid to avoid errors in the right or left direction, the number of notches to be racked, and the number of courses to be knitted between racking. Care must also be taken that the needles are never opposite each other when knitting on both beds simultaneously, as they can be seriously damaged. It may be necessary to rack the beds a half-pitch, depending on the design. Racking has a tendency to stretch the yarn, which therefore must be selected to be strong and flexible.

In hand-knitting, racking of the needlebeds corresponds to the crossing of stitches using a supplementary needle, a technique covered with cabled stitches in chapter 11.

Page 177

1 – Racking face and reverse.

2, 4, 5 – Zig-zags in the vertical direction.

3 – Fancy zig-zag edging.

6 – Chevron edging at cast-on edge (or at cast-off edge).

7, 8 – Pattern of straight wales together with racked wales, face and reverse.

9 – Three-dimensional effect in edging created by opposing racking over tuck ribs.

Page 178

10, 13, 16, 19 – Racking with openwork effects.

11, 14 – Ruching created with held stitches and racking: face and reverse.

17 – Structure similar to the sample described above, face and reverse: it also has contrasting stripes and tuck stitches.

12 – Racked rib with inlay.

15 – Racked rib with plating.

18 – Tubular knitting with racking.

20 – Double-face fabric with racking.

21 – Racked tubular knitting with one face in Lycra.

Page 180 – Double-face fabric with floats and racking.

11 Transfer stitches

A transfer stitch is one that has been moved from one needle to another one nearby, either to left or right on the same needlebed, or onto the opposite needlebed.

Transferring one or more stitches, tucks or held loops onto neighbouring needles enables the creation of textural surfaces, openwork fabrics and other effects:

1. transfer – rack – transfer. In this case, if the empty needle collects the yarn on the following course, it will form a new stitch and create a hole in this position (see chapter 12).

2. transfer – rack – transfer – rack – transfer. In this case, superimposing the stitches creates textured relief effects (see below).

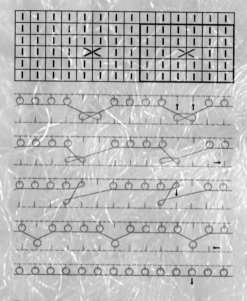

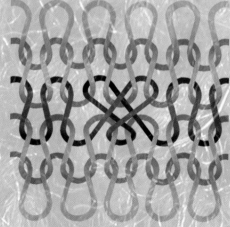

Stitches crossed to the right, face

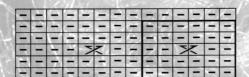

Reverse

Relief textures with crossed stitches

When stitches cross over each other, they lengthen and slant to the right or left, producing raised diagonal lines and waves of varying depths (depending on the yarn used, the tension, the number of stitches crossed, and the arrangement of the crossings). This results in cabled vertical structures (usually accentuated by reverse jersey fabric at the sides), or wavy textures, and diagonal lines (chevrons, lozenges, honeycomb patterns, woven effects or basket-weave, for example).

In the industry, transfer stitches are now made much more efficiently. Previously, it was necessary to make several empty traverses of the carriage, without knitting, which slowed down production and also increased the cost of the article.

On current domestic machines, these structures are made manually using two transfer tools with one, two or three points. The crossing of stitches is made to the right or left, over two, three or more needles, up to eight. When crossings are attempted over more than three stitches, the operation becomes impossible as the size of the stitches is not sufficient to reach the new position. Therefore the alternatives are:

- to manually knit a supplementary course, very loosely, across the relevant stitches, before the transfer operation, using a piece of yarn identical to the knitting, and knot it afterwards on the wrong side.
- to knit extra loops during the preceding course on needles of the opposite bed, then drop them, before transferring stitches. This technique is used in industry. However, recent machines have the ability to change the stitch length with precision across a single course, which makes these structures much easier to knit and improves their appearance.

In hand-knitting, crossings are usually made on the right side of the knitting. For example:

- for a crossing of two stitches to the right (one over one): knit into the second stitch on the needle, knitting into the front, then knit the first stitch.
- for a crossing of two stitches to the left (one over one): knit the second stitch on the needles, knitting into the back, then knit the first stitch.
- for a crossing of more than two stitches, use an additional double-pointed cable needle: slip one, two, or three (or more) stitches onto the cable needle, hold this needle in waiting in front of the knitting for a left crossing (or behind for a right crossing), knit the next stitch (or two or three or more), then knit the stitches from the cable needle.

Aran knitting (the name of an island in Ireland) is a regularly recurring trend in knitwear design. It consists of different structures based on purl fabrics, crossed and cabled stitches, and tuck stitches, generally worked together in vertical bands. New versions of this perennial favourite could be created by experimenting with different types of composition.

Knitted relief patterns can also be plated. If a design has been programmed, the knitting can be made as a jacquard of two or more colours. It can contain tuck stitches, floats or lace holes, so why not consider combining it with intarsia, partial knitting and other techniques?

Page 187 (1) – On a reverse jersey ground, crossing three knit stitches over three knit stitches, to the left, every four courses.

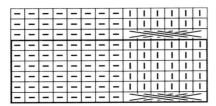

Page 187 (2) – On a reverse jersey ground, crossing to the left every two courses, one knit stitch over two knit stitches.

Page 187 (3, 5) – Undulating texture created by juxtaposing cables, face and reverse.

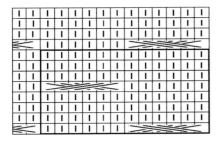

Page 187 (6) – Cables juxtaposed and reversed, to create a honeycomb texture.

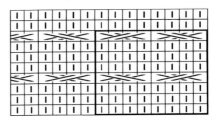

Page 187 (4) – On a reverse jersey ground, four successive crossings to the right, of one knit stitch over one knit stitch, every two courses.

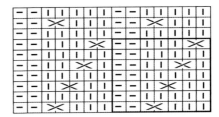

Page 188

7 – Interwoven structure created with a chainette yarn which is itself knitted and twisted.

8, 10, 12 – Fancy structured fabrics comprising knit stitches moving to the right and left on a reverse jersey ground.

9 – Aran style pattern comprising travelling cables, honeycomb and garter stitches.

11 – Vertical zig zags of knit stitches on a plain knit ground with crossings of two knit stitches over one, made to the right or left every two courses.

Page 191 (13 to 18) – Crossed stitches in two-colour float jersey jacquard.

Page 193 – Crossed stitches and partial knitting.

Page 194

19 – Same process with tucked stitches.

20 – Same process with cast-off stitches.

21 – Cables and float stitch.

12 Transfer lace and openwork stitches

These knitted fabrics are scattered with holes and are slightly textured because the stitches leaning to the left or right have been placed on top of another in order to be knitted together. The varied compositions often contain lattice effects, vertical, horizontal or diagonal stripes, zigzag patterns, diamond shapes, 'leaf' patterns, or all-over or placed designs.

In the knitting industry, transfer stitches used to be avoided as they slowed production down considerably. Some laces are less expensive than others; these are fabrics whose holes are immediately next to the stitches knitted together, as they require little extra movement. To produce transfer lace, two different techniques may be used: these are shown in the enlargements and drawings shown on pages 198 and 200. More elaborate laces incorporate holes that are some distance from the stitches knitted together, in which case the wales and courses of stitches are animated by curved or sloping movements with more pronounced textured effects. This particular feature is sometimes used to produce lace finishes along the width or length of a knitted fabric or braid. This lace is more costly because it requires many successive transfers prior to knitting.

For experimental purposes, on domestic machines transfers can be made manually using a transfer tool with one or more points; some machines have a special lace carriage, which operates on the back needlebed together with a programme. In general, graphs are recommended, but no instructions are given to encourage personal designs to be created. For information purposes, some examples of basic structures are shown on page 203 and page 204 (nos. 1 and 2).

On some machines, a programme is used just for the transfers, made in stages, and not for the knitting. After some courses of jersey, if the lace carriage is on the left:

- to transfer to the needles immediately to the left (knit side of jersey: slope to the right): pass the carriage from left to right, causing the selection of needles; then return the carriage, to bring about the transfer of the stitches from right to left.

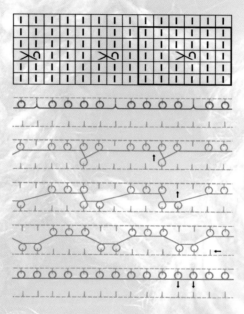

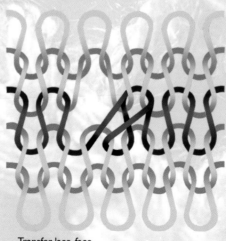

Transfer lace, face

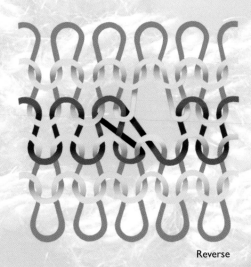

Reverse

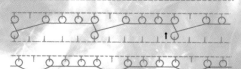

Transfer lace, right side

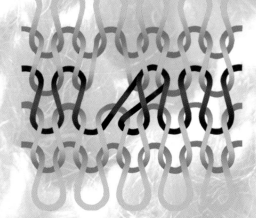

- to transfer to the needles immediately to the right (knit side of jersey: slope to left): the needle selection is first made from right to left and then the transfer from left to right (so the lace carriage must move to and fro twice before knitting).
- if the needle that holds two (or three) stitches following transfer needs to be further away from the momentarily empty needle, the stitches must be transferred in successive stages; each stage corresponds to the selection and movement of one stitch to the needle immediately next to it.

When the transfers are complete, the main carriage is used for knitting two or more courses of jersey, whether plain, striped, plated, or so on.

In the case of knitting an uneven number of courses, remember to set the main carriage to 'slip' and remove the yarn temporarily.

If an additional design has been inserted into the programming of the transfer pattern, the knitting can, of course, be carried out in two-colour jacquard (or more) with tucks and floats, by setting the main carriage accordingly (see the chapters concerned). However, it is often easier to knit one or more courses of jacquard and subsequently transfer stitches by hand.

In hand-knitting, transfer stitches knitted on the face (knit) side are obtained as follows:

- for a transfer sloping to the right: knit two stitches together then make one yarn over (this yarn over is made by winding the yarn once round the needle before knitting the next stitch).
- for a transfer sloping to the left, work as follows: yarn over, then slip one stitch knitways, knit the next stitch, then pass the slipped stitch over.
- for a double transfer of one stitch to the left and one stitch to the right underneath a central stitch: make one yarn over, then slip the next two stitches together (starting with the second), then slip the third, knit these three stitches together knitways and make another yarn over. In this case the number of stitches remains the same. Reminder: the yarn overs are not always situated immediately next to the transfer stitches.
- for a transfer sloping to the right on the face side but knitted from the reverse (purl) side of the fabric: make a yarn over and then purl two together. The other slopes are much more tricky. It is preferable to use an additional needle.

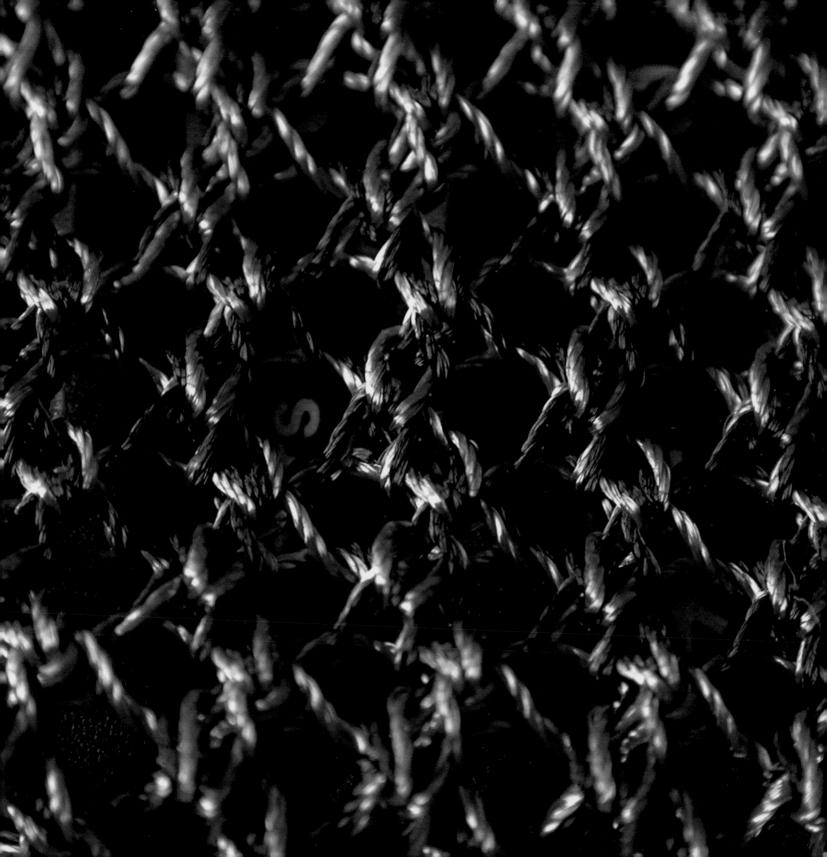

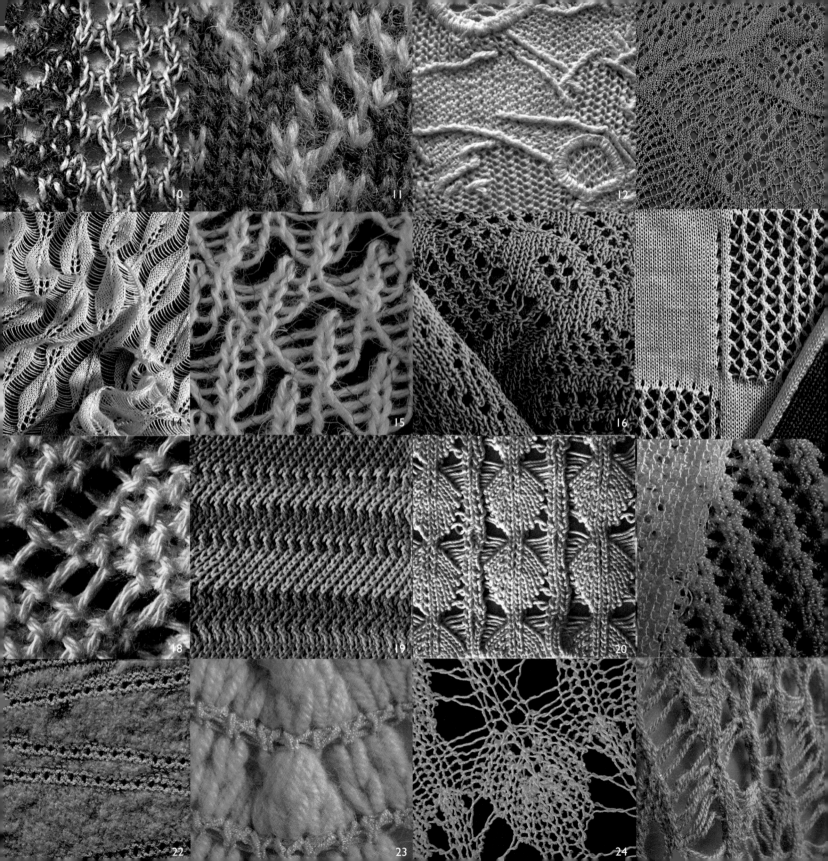

Lace on a jersey base:
The holes are adjacent to the transfer stitches.
Page 203 – The transfers are made either to the right or to the left alternately; the knitted stitches are perpendicular to the casting on.

Page 204
1 – The transfers are always made to the right: the knitted stitches are slanted diagonally.

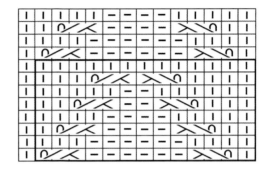

4 – Knit side of jersey, successive diagonal transfers to produce diamond-shape compositions.
7 – Gaps and raised stitches in zigzag patterns, knit side of jersey.
2 – Plain knit design on openwork ground.

The transfers are at a distance from the new wales created by holes:
5 – Pattern of leaves increasing in size, comprising knit stitches on a reverse jersey ground; the transfer stitches in each leaf motif gradually become further away from the holes.
8 – Pattern of textured curves emphasized by the presence of purl stitches.
3, 6 – The increases (whether visible or not) and decreases are grouped together locally: the courses are no longer in a straight line; they form a wavy effect or chevron pattern on the surface of the fabric, and also at the beginning and end of the panel.
9 – Transfer openwork design broken up by areas of reverse jersey.

Page 205 – Transfers and gaps made every course, right side and wrong side.

Page 206
10 – Plated openwork jersey, right side/wrong side.
14 – Openwork transfer and ladder stitches.
18 – Openwork transfer and tuck stitches.
22 – Transfer lace stripes and partial knitting.
11 – Two-colour float jacquard and transfer.
15 – Same technique with invisible yarn.
19 – Two-colour jacquard with transfers every course.
23 – Decreases and crossings at the same time.
12 – Composition with various structures and hand embroidery.
16, 20, 13, 17, 21 and 25 – Laces incorporating ribbed or double-faced areas.
24 – Same technique knitted with Lycra and viscose yarn.

Page 208 – Transfers with crossed stitches, openwork lace transfers and ladder stitches.

13 More stitches using transfers

'Opaque lace' or split stitch

Also known as 'closed' transfer patterning, this involves a process that transfers only half the stitch. This stitch is therefore held and knitted across two needles, which eliminates the gap at the start of the wale. This technique is also used in other processes, such as partial knitting for example, for the same reason, in order to eliminate holes.

Some domestic machines can produce similar effects with a special carriage setting ('shadow' or 'fine lace'). It is also possible to pick up half a stitch from the previous course onto a needle using a hand tool.

In hand-knitting there are several possible methods: knit a stitch twice, first knitwise then purlwise, or vice versa; pick up a stitch or a strand from a previous row on the face or reverse side; and so on. In every case, the exact method should be specified in a caption next to the graph as a reminder or for use in commercial patterns.

Gauge changes

It is worth remembering that eliminating or increasing stitches also makes it possible to effectively change gauge and therefore yarn count. For example, the knitting may start off in gauge 12 and then after transfers that eliminate one needle out of two, or two out of three, the knitting could continue in gauge 7 or 5 with a much coarser yarn. Some courses further on, all the needles can be brought back into action by using the split-stitch technique or another method.

This technique can be used to include stitches of different thickness in one section of a knitted panel to create particular effects. However, these differences in gauge remain subject to the capacity of the needles in terms of yarn count.

On both industrial and domestic machines, gauge changes will be more pronounced if one of the yarns used contains elastane.

In hand-knitting, gauge changes are easy and can be very spectacular. Simply change the needle size and the yarn count. The difficulty lies in controlling the width of the knit and the different densities. Therefore, several tests will be needed with different size needles.

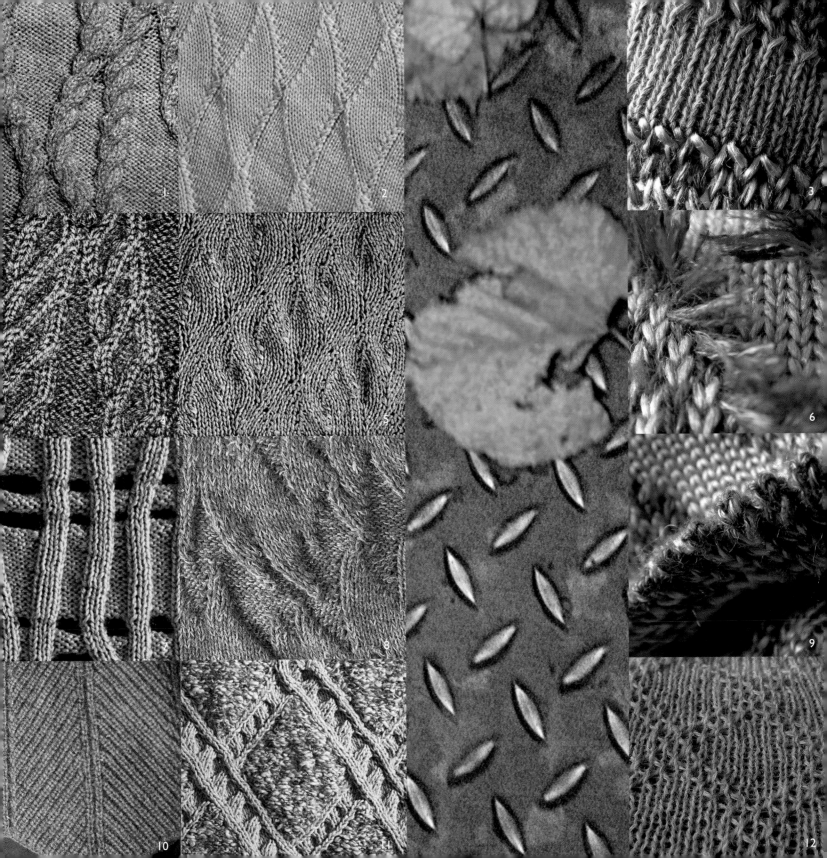

Fully-fashioned knitting

Products that consist of panels whose borders match the shape of the garment pattern are produced on Cotton straight bar machines and on the new, flat-bed machines. The front upper bed on some four-bed machines is split into two segments. The lateral movement of each of the parts is therefore independent and it enables increases or decreases to be produced within the panel itself without lengthening the production time.

Picking up the yarn on an empty needle (or making a yarn over) also involves creating a new wale and, therefore, making an increase. Conversely, knitting two stitches together after transfer results in a decrease.

When increases or decreases are produced a few needles away from the selvedge, the marks resulting from these operations (a slight gap from increases and the raised double stitch of the transfer resulting from decreases) form lines parallel to the shaped edges of the piece. These characteristics are the hallmark of fully-fashioned knitting.

Placed across the width of a knitted fabric, successive increases or decreases can be used to produce fabrics with very large textured stitches, and also fabrics with circular, hexagonal or other shapes whose stitch courses no longer run in a straight line but concentrically. Therefore, these knitted forms can be of limitless shape. Usually, this technique is used to make caps, berets, lace tablecloths, special necks, etc.

Fully fashioned shaping remained for a long time the prerogative of hand-knitting but, now, recent machines are designed to achieve these effects or to produce shaped knitting for volumetric pieces (three-dimensional knitting). These techniques have led to the creation and development of 'seamless' industrial knitting.

13   14
15   16
17   18
19   20

Page 213
1, 2, 4, 5, 7, 8, 10 – 'Opaque lace' or the use of 'split
stitch' (a method that conceals the gaps).
1, 4 – Curved cables.
7 – Transfer with cast-off stitches.
11 – Intarsia jacquard – the cables are on a single
jersey base, the diamonds are double face.

3, 6, 9 – Transferring enables the gauge to be changed.
6 – Transferring allows floats to be made on the right
side, which are then cut.
9 – Sample of finishing with transfer.
12 – Partial transfer or 'shadow lace'.

Page 214 – Two-colour tuck rib with discreet increases
and transfers.
Pages 216–217
13 – Increases and decreases at the selvedge.
14, 18, 20 – Decreases moving towards the centre.
15, 17 – Fully fashioned, decreases close to the
selvedge.
16 – Increases moving away from the centre.
19 – Decreases across the width of the knitting
(for example between the cables).
21, 22 – Decreasing within the interior of a panel.

14 Fine-gauge fabrics

Basic rib structure and basic interlock structure

These come under the category of 'knitted fabrics by the roll' and are also known as 'jersey knit fabrics'.

These are fabrics created from both simple and complex structures produced mainly on fine and extremely fine-gauge machines. The stitches are therefore hardly visible. These textiles account for some 60 to 70 per cent of production in the hosiery industry. Produced by continuous knitting, they are intended for making up cut-and-sew articles. They are knitted on circular machines with one or two needlebeds, which can therefore knit plain (single) jersey, or double jersey rib and interlock structures. Fine gauges are most common, with a high proportion being between 20 and 28 gauge.

The machines operate without programming. They have one or two beds, which are equipped with needles having butts at several possible levels (1 to 5 on single-bed machines and, as a general rule, 2 on double-bed machines. Beyond that, it is preferable to use jacquard or mini-jacquard systems for selecting needles).

The needles, which are arranged to produce a given stitch structure, are controlled at each feeder (the equivalent of a carriage) by one or other of the butts, which means that at each feeder, on a double-bed machine, it is possible to activate either the long needles or the short ones (i.e. with the butt close to or far from the hook).

Most of the fabrics shown in the previous chapters that have been knitted on jersey and rib structure single- or double-bed machines can be transposed onto circular fine-gauge machines, except for those that require stitch movements obtained by racking.

Among the double-bed machines, attention should be drawn to the special type of interlock machine, in which the needles of the two beds are arranged opposite each other, but they only work alternately, when the needle opposite is out of action. The basic structures therefore consist of inter-linked ribs (for example, two 1 x 1 interlinked ribs form the basic interlock knitted fabric; if two 2 x 2 ribs interlink, this is referred to as a '2 x 2' interlock structure).

Among the complex structures produced on interlock machines, attention is drawn to so-called 'eight-lock' knitted fabrics. These consist of combinations of entire or partial courses of ribs and jersey, as well as combinations of interlock and jersey courses. In both cases, the presence of tuck, float and elongated stitches reduces the number of courses and changes the visual and behavioural character-istics of the fabrics. Coloured effects (wide or fine stripes, mini-checks, and so on) can also be produced.

Jersey, rib and interlock fine knitted fabrics can be created with all kinds of yarns (spun fibre yarn, continuous filament yarns, a combination of knitted elastic yarns, plated yarns). In some cases, they behave almost like fabrics that do not unravel.

Some manual semi-industrial machines operate in the same way. Some needles have high butts and others low butts, and these are selected as the carriage passes.

In hand-knitting, the procedure is the same as that used for double-face fabrics (see chapter 8).

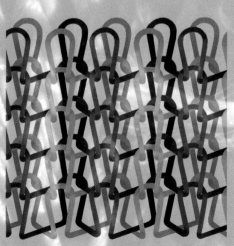

1 x 1 interlock

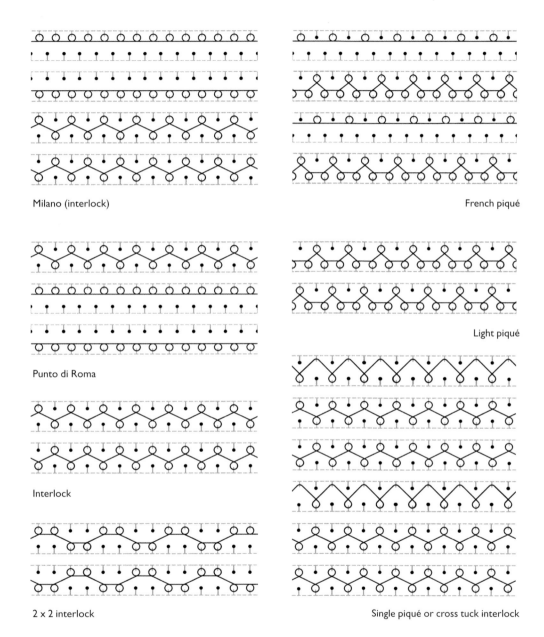

Milano (interlock)

French piqué

Punto di Roma

Light piqué

Interlock

2 x 2 interlock

Single piqué or cross tuck interlock

15 Stitch variations

This chapter shows a number of variations on standard structures created on double-bed machines, using techniques discussed in previous chapters.

Little structured stitches

These consist of all-over self patterned designs over a small repeat (i.e. only a few stitches and rows) developed by combining two or more of the structures explained above (stitches of several colours and purl, tuck, float, slip, transfer and other stitches). Even though a number of these structures are already well known, when used with new materials they can almost seem to be reinvented. Very often they are reversible and therefore can be used in larger repeats, incorporating both face and reverse effects on the same side.

Combining several technically compatible small structures into larger compositions requires great care to perfect. Depending on the yarn count, stitch setting and materials used, the results obtained will be discreet but subtle and refined.

On semi-industrial manual machines, to combine programming and the use of the hand tool, change the mechanical settings and also perhaps, change carriage every other course, are operations that can be highly complex and therefore, for some designs, there should be no hesitation in resorting to hand-knitting.

For experimentation in hand-knitting, it is preferable to use double-pointed needles so that it is easier to change and handle the yarns. It is also advisable to note each stage on a graph and repeat an effect several times.

Tuck ribs

The term 'tuck rib' is used to refer to full needle ribs with tucks on one face. Just as on a single-bed machine, the number of tucks on the same needle is limited; it varies according to the yarn count used and the stitch length settings. On the opposite side to the tucks, the wales of plain stitches ripple around these marked tuck stitches, which are wider and heavier than plain stitches. Just as on a single-bed machine, knitted fabrics incorporating many tucks are generally supple and have a lively texture.

On domestic machines, these effects are produced quite simply with a needle selection programmed on the back bed. On this bed, the carriage is set to 'tuck'. It is also possible to create a tuck by picking up a stitch lower down the wale onto a hand tool, allowing the stitches above to run down to the hand tool and then placing all the floats obtained in this way onto the needle corresponding to the wale, and knitting them all together.

In hand-knitting, proceed as for knitting beaded ribs, arranging the tucks in a larger repeat.

Knops

Knopped knitted fabrics are variations on tuck ribs. As they accumulate, the tucks push aside the adjacent stitches, forming a hollow and a gap. At the same time, the wales knitted on the other bed form embossed textures: knots or knops. The racking of the beds enables certain knopped characteristics to be emphasized. These knits are often reversible. They are created in the same way as the tuck ribs.

Three-dimensional knops or 'bobbles' can also be created with partial knitting (see chapter 5); the relief effects are emphasized by increasing the number of stitches in one place before the partial knitting and then decreasing again (for example, knitting three or five stitches in one stitch and, after a few rows, casting off these stitches onto a single one). Bobbles are most often created using manual machine-knitting or by hand.

Ripples and ridges

Ripples (or bourrelets) are created on a ground of 1 x 1 rib or full needle rib or fancy rib (or rib jacquard; see chapter 16), by knitting several courses in plain jersey, jersey jacquard or other fabric on one bed, while the stitches on the opposite bed are held.

Ottomans are knitted (or woven) fabrics that incorporate regular ridges or ripples. These knitted textiles are produced in very fine gauges, but they are nevertheless compact and heavy.

While knitting the ripple on one bed, the knitted fabric is held in suspense on the other bed. The additional courses of stitches are not weighted and therefore they are limited in number depending on the yarn count and the stitch dial setting. In the knitting industry, flat-bed machines fitted with a presser-foot are able to accumulate a much larger number of courses. On single-bed circular machines, the sinker plates encourage the formation of ripple effects.

These knitted fabrics may also incorporate floats or openwork stitches, or may be racked or inlaid.

On domestic machines, which are flat bed, the stitches are held, preferably on the front bed, while the courses are accumulating on the back bed. It is advisable to manually bring out the needles to position D and sometimes even temporarily insert a cast-on comb in the ripple being formed.

Chapter 3 showed that ridged effects can also be produced on plain jersey fabric by picking up the stitch heads of a previous course of stitches onto the needles using a hand tool.

In hand-knitting, it is necessary to pick up a stitch situated several rows away and knit it with the corresponding stitch in the current row being formed. Then, simply repeat this operation regularly or occasionally, depending on the desired effect. To work more accurately and avoid counting rows, it is possible to position markers by hand, as on a machine: at the starting point of the ripple, knit together with a strong contrast yarn. Once the ripple has been closed, this temporary yarn can be removed by pulling on it.

11   12   13

For reasons of weight and comfort, ripples are generally incorporated selectively into hand-knitted garments.

Fancy ripples or ridged fabrics

These knitted fabrics are produced in full needle ribs with programming. Some needles are selected to knit and others are held while the courses are accumulating on the opposite bed. This produces double-knit raised effects on a 1 x 1 rib ground. The designs appear in relief, and may include interrupted ripples, diagonal or zigzag patterns, or wavy effects. These textiles are heavy, compact and not very stretchy, so it is preferable to knit them with plain, thin, fine-gauge yarns.

On domestic machines, these knits are made with a programme that makes a needle selection and by setting the carriage on that side to 'slip'.

To be hand-knitted, these textiles must be lightened as much as possible, using thin yarn, loose tension, widely spaced ripple effects, and so on.

Ripples on the reverse side of plain jersey

Ridges always used to be made in relief on the face side of plain jersey. On the new generation of machines, the presser plates are used to produce textured stitches on the reverse side of the jersey. These textiles incorporate straight across and regular ripples, although diagonal, progressively thicker, discontinuous and other ripple patterns may also occur. They are obtained by knitting with alternate needles with the intermediate needles each holding one stitch out of action.

These effects are difficult to reproduce on domestic machines. Some effects may, however, be created by over-embroidering with Swiss darning once the knitting is finished. It is also possible to use the metal hooks that are positioned on the bed between each needle to temporarily transfer and hold one or more stitches (and even a half-stitch). The process is fairly tricky and it is therefore advisable to bring out the needles to position D while knitting the ripples. Then, using a latch tool, pick up the stitches out of action on the adjacent needles while at the same time holding the knitting downwards. At this stage, again bring out the needles to position D prior to knitting.

In hand-knitting, knit- or purl-faced ripples are obtained in the same way. Another way of obtaining a purl ripple with slipped stitches is as follows: (*) purl one, yarn forward, slip the next stitch as it is (*), and repeat from (*) to (*), avoid tightening. The next row: (*) yarn back, slip the same stitch as previous row, (*) knit one stitch and repeat from (*) to (*). Repeat these steps over several rows.

Drop-stitch fabrics

These knitted fabrics generally consist of jersey and 'dropped' stitches either singly or in groups every course or every two or more courses. Recent industrial machines are able to accurately adjust the stitch length and tension on particular groups of needles, and so do not need to drop the stitches in order to obtain these openwork effects.

On the oldest machines and on domestic machines, the dropped stitches are temporarily held on the second bed (through programming or manually) and then released immediately or after knitting several courses. The yarn released in this way enlarges the selected group of stitches of the main fabric, creating distortions, transparencies or floats, depending on the needle layout. The knitted fabric produced in this way is flexible and light.

As has been mentioned, this method is also used to produce some kinds of cable stitch, prior to transferring stitches, on those machines that do not have the facility to change the stitch length.

In hand-knitting, temporary stitches are formed by 'yarn overs', which are knitted over a number of rows and then deliberately dropped.

Dropped stitches and cast-off stitches

Just as on single-bed machines, in double-knit fabric some stitches can be dropped or cast off and others cast on several courses later. Holes of various sizes allow the reverse side of the jersey fabric ground, or variation, to show through. On the face side, these dropped or cast-off stitches roll up, forming a pronounced curve. All around, the fabric is double-face rib or rib jacquard.

If this principle is combined with partial knitting, it is possible to envisage much larger three-dimensional effects, whether of even or uneven width, in jersey, jersey derivatives or ribs. Shapes are knitted separately and then transferred onto the stitches of the ground, cast off or dropped. These textured stitches can also be knitted into the ground from time to time, possibly also racking the beds.

Amazing structures and finishings can be created in this way, such as pockets knitted at the same time as the garment.

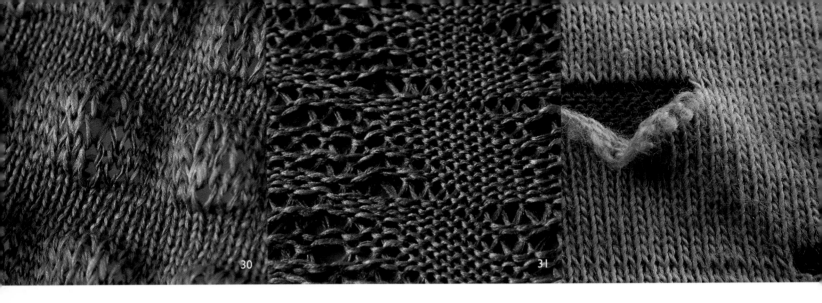

30

31

On domestic machines, proceed as on single-bed machines: create the effects by manually casting off and casting on. In hand-knitting, the dropped stitches are difficult to maintain. All the handling quickly causes the stitches to run.

Structured transfer patterns with stitches alternately present and 'absent'

The term 'transfer patterns' is often used to refer to purl stitch fabrics, though it can also apply to knits composed of stitches that start on one face with a tuck loop and then disappear a few rows later, knitted into the ground. These fabrics therefore include some areas knitted on single bed and other areas knitted on double bed. On the face side, their texture in double-knit jersey appears on a self-coloured, plated or striped reverse jersey background incorporating floats or tucks.

On one of the beds, all (or almost all) the needles are in action; tucks are made between these stitches on the other bed and then transferred onto the needles of the first bed some courses later. Over these few rows, these loops may be knitted in jersey, held, ribbed, racked, etc.

On manual semi-industrial machines, the needles are put into action and then, after a few courses, according to the pattern, manually transferred onto the opposite bed. As it is impossible to see and assess the progress of the work between the two beds, it is necessary to work according to a pre-prepared drawing on a graph.

In hand-knitting, extra stitches are made with a yarn over or by picking up a thread from the previous row, or else by knitting a stitch twice (knitwise and then purlwise, or vice versa).

This list of stitch variations is far from comprehensive. It will be enhanced further with yarn changes in coloured jacquards in the next chapter.

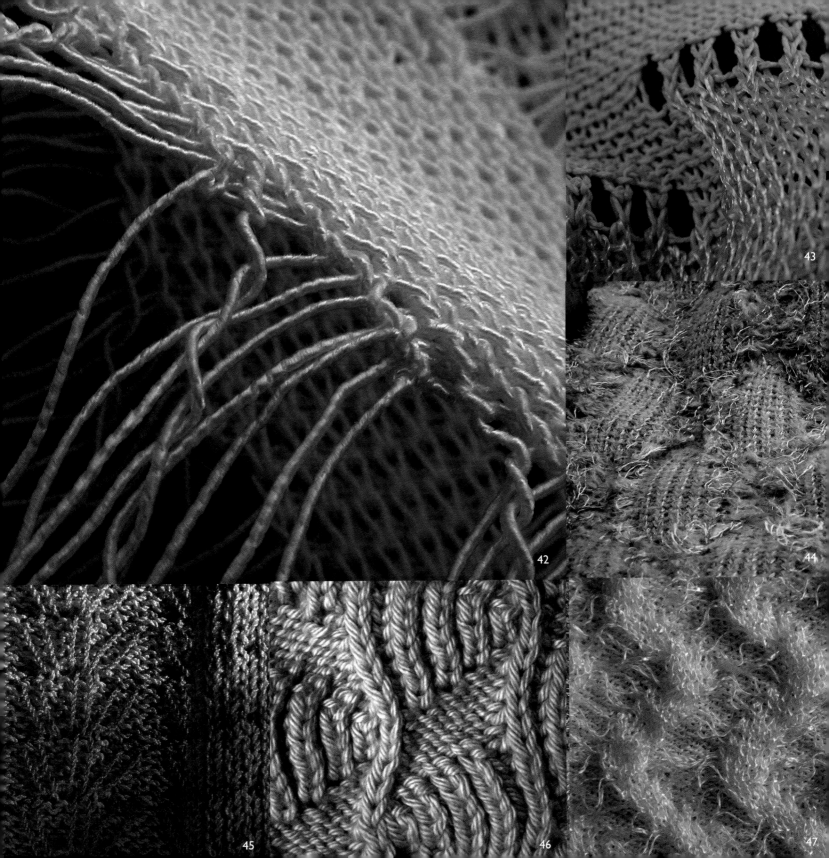

42

43

44

45

46

47

60

61

62

16 'Composite' stitches Multicolour jacquards

Colour jacquards produced with two needlebeds are very different from jersey jacquards, as they are knitted on a rib or double-knit structure. These knitted fabrics do not roll up; they tend to be heavier and less supple: the greater the number of colours per course, the heavier the textile becomes. As a general rule, jacquards are therefore knitted in fine and medium gauges. Jacquards can technically incorporate a fairly large number of colours per course, but, for reasons of cost and flexibility of the end product, it is rare to exceed four colours on circular machines and six on flat-bed machines.

Some jacquards can be produced on domestic machines with usually two colours per course, though sometimes even three or four. Colours that appear in small quantities can be embroidered by hand (see chapter 4).

In hand-knitting, a great deal of patience is required, just as in knitting double-face fabrics.

There are several types of rib jacquard (see chapter 8).

Double jacquard

On the reverse side or backing, all the stitches are knitted with each traverse of the carriage. This knit is therefore not balanced since, for one jacquard face course, two are knitted on the reverse side. For a jacquard with three colours per course, one design course corresponds to three courses on the reverse side. This causes elongation of the stitches on the face side and ripples on the backing. On the face, the stitches hardly cover the purl stitches of the backing, which 'grin' through.

On hand flat machines, which have only one and not two feeders, with a crossed yarn guide (a colour changer only on one side), two courses are knitted on the back needlebed, while four courses are knitted on the front bed.

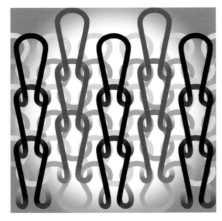

Double jacquard, face side

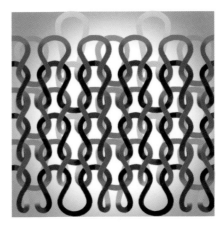

Reverse side

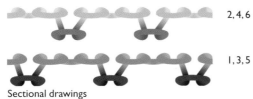

2, 4, 6

1, 3, 5

Sectional drawings

2, 4, 6

1, 3, 5

Diagrammatic representation

Graph representation   face side

I	I	I	I	I	I	I	I	I	I	I	I	I
I	I	I	I	I	I	I	I	I	I	I	I	I
I	I	I	I	I	I	I	I	I	I	I	I	I
I	I	I	I	I	I	I	I	I	I	I	I	I
I	I	I	I	I	I	I	I	I	I	I	I	I

reverse

I	V	I	V	I	V	I	V	I	V	I	V
V	I	V	I	V	I	V	I	V	I	V	I
I	V	I	V	I	V	I	V	I	V	I	V
V	I	V	I	V	I	V	I	V	I	V	I
I	V	I	V	I	V	I	V	I	V	I	V

1

2

3

4

Birdseye jacquard

On the reverse side, with each pass of the carriage, only every alternate stitch is knitted, changing selection each traverse. With two colours per design row, this knit is balanced, as it incorporates the same number of stitches on the reverse side as on the face. However, for a jacquard with four colours per design row, one course on the face side corresponds to two on the reverse. The structure of the reverse side or backing affects the appearance of the face side. On the face, the stitches tend to slant both to the right and the left, creating a slightly textured piqué effect. The term 'birdseye' that is used to describe this jacquard derives from the single stitch pattern of the backing.

Some manual machines can be set to knit alternately every other stitch on the front needlebed.

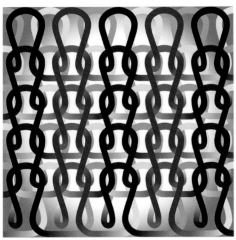

Birdseye jacquard, face side

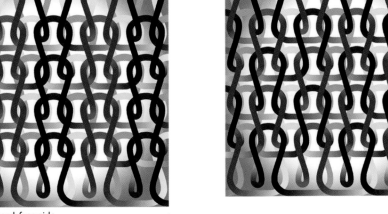

Reverse side

Sectional drawings

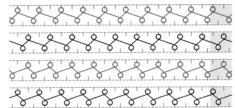

Diagrammatic representation

reverse   face

Graph representation

5

8

9

Double-face jacquard

Double-face jacquards have the same design on the face side and the reverse side, positive on one side and negative on the other. If there are large areas of one colour, the knit forms a pocket. It is also possible to produce two different designs on each of the faces, using one common yarn and a different yarn for each of the jacquards. In very fine gauge, two independent jacquards can be linked together by tucks with a linking yarn, just as with self-coloured double-face fabrics. The ability to programme a design on each face of the knit means that the striped or birdseye backing of rib jacquards is remodelled. On the majority of manual machines, selection of needles on the front bed can only be made manually. It is therefore easier and faster to knit two jacquards separately and assemble them with an unobtrusive yarn.

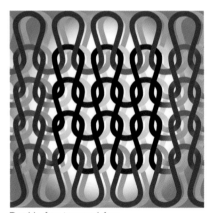

Double-face jacquard, face

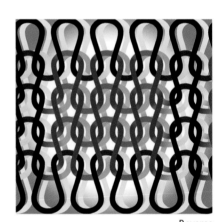

Reverse

1, 5

2, 3, 4

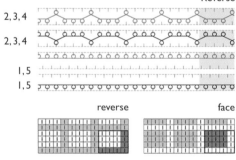

2, 3, 4

2, 3, 4

1, 5

1, 5

reverse   face

11

12 13 14 15

Blister or relief jacquard

This is generally made with two colours per course. The yarn of the design is knitted in jersey and the ground yarn in ribbing. When the design yarn is not knitted, it floats, held between the rib courses. The reverse side or backing of the fabric is self-coloured in ground yarn. Blister jacquards are usually produced on fine-gauge machines. Increasingly, the blister is emphasized by using an elastane or similar yarn for knitting the ribbed ground.

On manual machines, this jacquard is obtained by setting the front carriage to 'slip' when it knits with the design yarn and to 'knit' when it is knitting the ground.

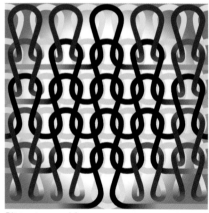

Blister jacquard face

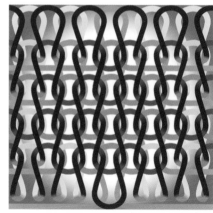

Reverse or backing

3

2, 4

1, 5

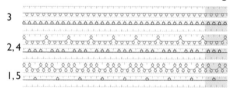

3

2, 4

1, 5

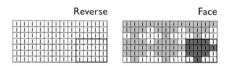

Reverse   Face

25

26

28

29

31

32

Transfer jacquard

This jacquard consists of areas of single-bed jacquard and areas of double-bed jacquard. On the jacquard side, the selected needles are pushed into action as they are needed (as in chapter 15). These extra stitches, which make up the pattern, are knitted in single, birdseye or double-face jacquard and then transferred onto the opposite bed, according to the composition of the design. Around the pattern, the ground stitches appear as reverse jersey stripes, or with floats or tuck stitches. These jacquard fabrics are, of course, much more supple and lighter than the previous ones. This technique is therefore now also used to lighten the backing of rib jacquards.

On manual machines, transfer jacquards are made by programming the design and then using a hand tool to transfer the stitches from one needlebed to the other.

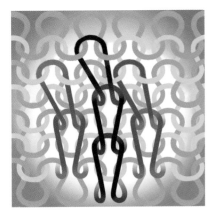

Transfer jacquard, face

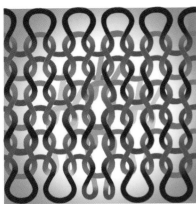

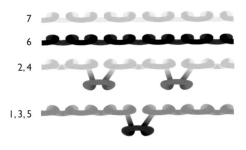

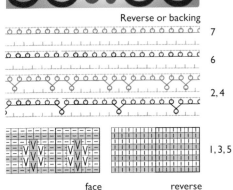

Reverse or backing

face   reverse

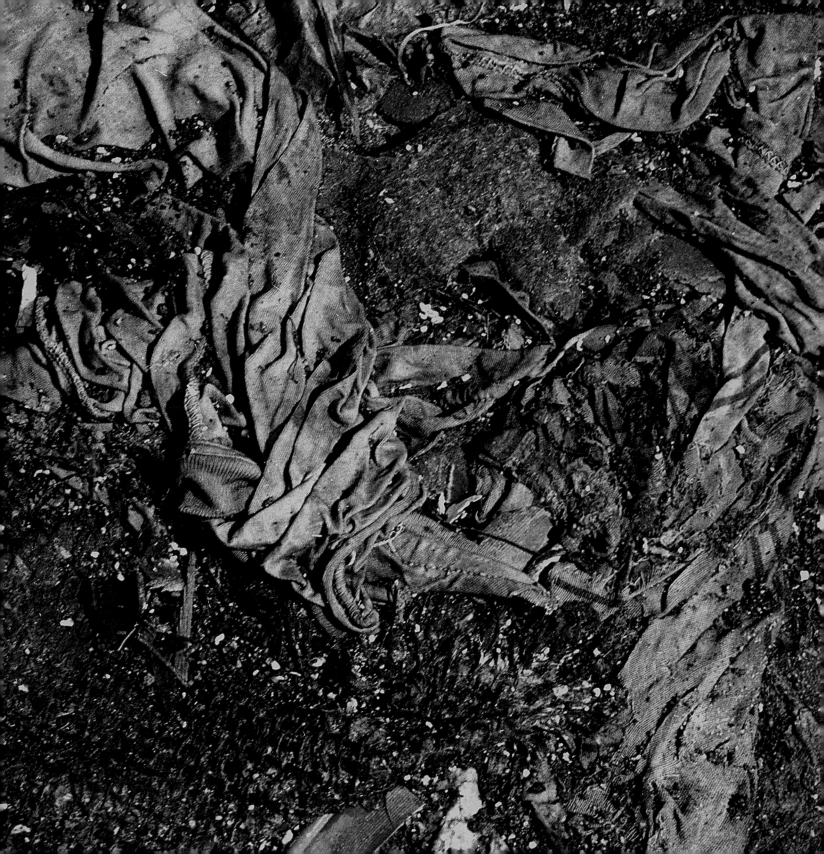

Fancy jacquards

The jacquards described above can be combined and further developed by removing wales, knitting for longer in certain areas, using racking, transfers, and so on.

Intarsia

Just as for intarsia in jersey, intarsia in ribbing is a method that can be used to increase the number of colours in one course without adding to the weight and thickness of the fabric. The yarns only appear in their own field according to the requirements of the design. In addition, on some machines, intarsia knits can incorporate highly varied structures, and may combine in one panel all the jacquards that have been described for both single and double needlebed. These new technical possibilities allow great control over the appearance of face and reverse, and the weight and suppleness of the fabrics.

Manufacturers of domestic machines have not made provision for intarsia using the double needlebed. Sampling rib intarsia is therefore tricky and rather a lengthy process, though not impossible, at least, not for some types of designs.

Recent achievements, incorporating the use of three-dimensional knitting and partial knitting with intarsia, have overcome all the traditional constraints of weft knitting.

45

46

47

48

49

50

Page 251 – Double jacquard with striper backing: the yarns form stripes on the reverse side.
1 – Jacquard with four colours per course, produced with only one feeder; face and reverse.
2 – Jacquard with two colours per course, produced with only one feeder; this knit is made lighter on the reverse.
3 – Jacquard with four colours per course; face and reverse; produced with two feeders and crossed yarn guide.
4 – Jacquard with two colours per course, produced with only one feeder; face and reverse; every alternate needle of the backing has been removed.

Page 254 – Birdseye jacquard: on the backing, the stitches are knitted alternately.
5 – Jacquard with three colours per course.
6 – Jacquard with four colours per course; the face has then been brushed.
7 – Jacquard with six colours per course.
8, 9, 10 – The new three- and four-colour jacquards are lightened by a selection on the reverse side which takes into account the design.
10 – The ground colours incorporate Lycra.

Page 257 – Double-face jacquard.
11, 12 – Face and reverse.
13, 14 – Face and reverse; knitted with one viscose yarn and one yarn with Lycra.
15 – Jacquard incorporating two different, small two-colour designs on each face.

Page 259 – Blister jacquard; the reverse side is self-coloured.
16 – The ground is livened up with a piqué effect.
17 – Jacquard produced with two yarns of very different counts.
18, 19 – The design is knitted with a larger number of courses than the ground.
20, 21 – Two-colour jacquard, with the relief effect accentuated by using a yarn incorporating Lycra.
22 – The texture is enhanced by racking the needlebeds.
23 – Giant felted floats.
24 – Large cut floats.

Page 260 – Transfer jacquards; the structure incorporating some areas knitted on one needlebed and others knitted on two needlebeds.
25, 26, 29 – Two-colour jacquard, with floats.
27 – Three-colour jacquard and floats.
28 – Same process used on the reverse side in order to control the floats that are too long.
30 – Transfer jacquard and partial knitting.
31 – Structured jacquard, partial knitting with racking and knops.
32 – Transfer jacquard and racking; the relief emphasized by using a Lycra yarn on the reverse side.
33 – Transfer jacquard, crossed stitches and transfer openwork stitches.

Page 262 – Transfer jacquard, ripples and partial knitting.

Page 265 – Fancy jacquards
34, 35 – Double-face and two-colour fisherman's ribs.
36 – Same process.
37 – Double-face jacquard with three colours per course, with beaded ribs.
38 – Jacquard with three colours per course, with ripples in some areas.
39 – Two-colour double-face and openwork stitches.
40 – Two-colour birdseye jacquard and transfer stitches; one of the yarns is 'transparent'.
41 – Double-face and crossed stitches.
42, 43 – Jacquard and partial knitting.
44 – Double-face and racking.

Page 267 – Intarsias
45, 46 – Intarsia and ladder stitch, face and reverse.
47 – Birdseye jacquard knitted with a transparent nylon yarn.
48 – Double-face jacquard, stitches cast off and cast on over a group of needles.
49 – Patchwork with eight colours per course, knitted using purl stitches, cable stitches and two-colour jersey jacquard.
50 – Ribs with partial knitting and transfers.

17 Speciality stitches

The stitches described in this chapter are produced on single needlebed circular machines and they come under the category of 'knitted fabrics by the metre' or fine-gauge jersey products described in chapter 14.

They are different from knits most commonly used for their face side (knit face) because here it is the reverse side that has the more interesting characteristics and appearance.

Plush (or knitted terry) jersey

This is produced by knitting two yarns at the same time: one is used exclusively as a ground yarn (it is often a fine, shrinkable yarn; for example, a textured synthetic yarn), while the other forms loops at the foot of the stitches on the reverse side of the jersey. On industrial machines, these loops are obtained through the perpendicular movement of the sinker plates in an arrangement referred to as a sinker-wheel. A solution on double-bed machines is to use the needles of the second needlebed as elements to pick up the loops and then drop them. This technique requires the machines to be specially adapted. Therefore, it is preferable to use plush or terry machines, which are specially designed for this purpose.

The plush effect can be produced uniformly over the whole fabric, or a design can be created in relief on a reverse jersey background (jacquard plush).

In the knitting industry, it is possible to produce this structure in jacquard with two or more colours per course. Some fabrics also incorporate loops on both face and reverse sides (double-face plush).

This technique is particularly used to manufacture babywear and sportswear.

Some manual double-bed machines can produce plush jersey with a single yarn per course. The knits are therefore self-coloured or striped. With a selection of needles on the back needlebed, it is also possible to obtain designs in relief. After the traverse of the main carriage, an additional small but highly efficient carriage is used to drop the loops after each course.

In hand-knitting, to produce giant loops where required, the yarn is held round one (or more) fingers while knitting the two yarns together.

Plush jersey can also be used as a base stitch, to produce textiles of highly varied and, at times, rather spectacular appearance.

Fleecy fabric

These knits are produced by inlay on a jersey ground. The floats vary in length on the reverse side and are then brushed.

They are produced with a fluffy inlay yarn, the surface of which is raised by a light or heavy brushing action. The texture of the knit stitches softens or disappears completely.

Stronger or lighter brushing can also be applied to various other knitted fabrics; for example, to the reverse (or face) of plain jersey fabric, to a single jersey with slipped stitches (and therefore floats), to inlaid fabrics or to plush jerseys and interlocks.

On a small scale, brushing is done manually using stiff brushes.

Polar fleece

Polar fleece is obtained by brushing both sides of double- and single-face plush fabrics.

Velvet

On very fine-gauge circular machines, the knitting is carried out in plush jersey and then the loops are sheared. These textiles may also undergo other finishing treatments, including creasing, pressing and various printing processes.

(Another process is used in warp knitting: this is by knitting two fabrics face to face, which are linked together by the yarn, and then separated by cutting.)

Velvets may be single colour, striped or jacquard.

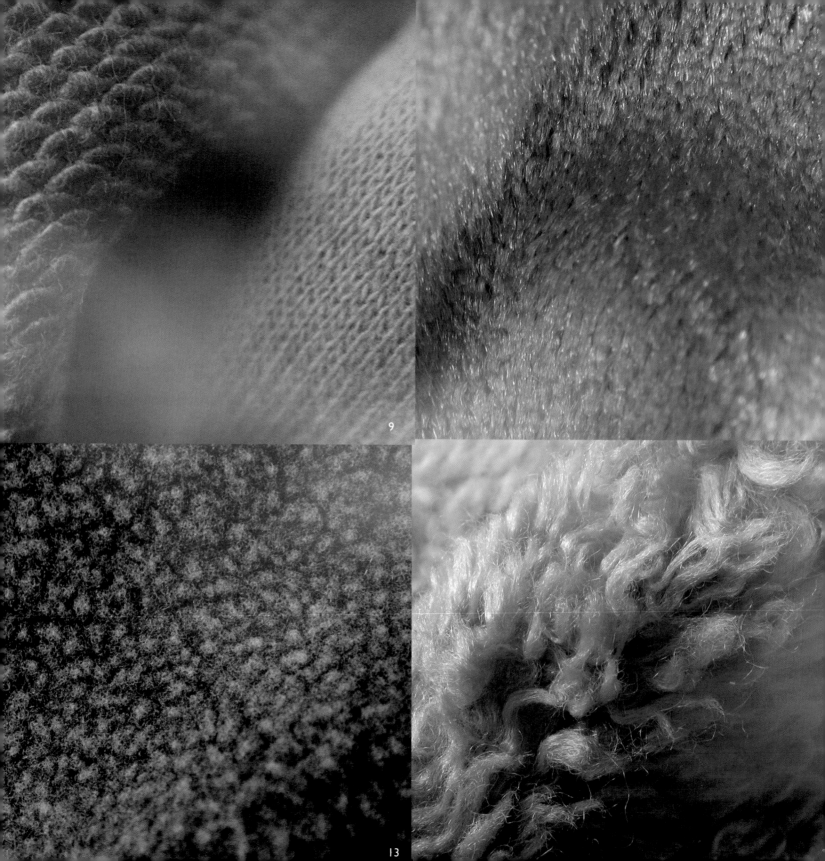

9

13

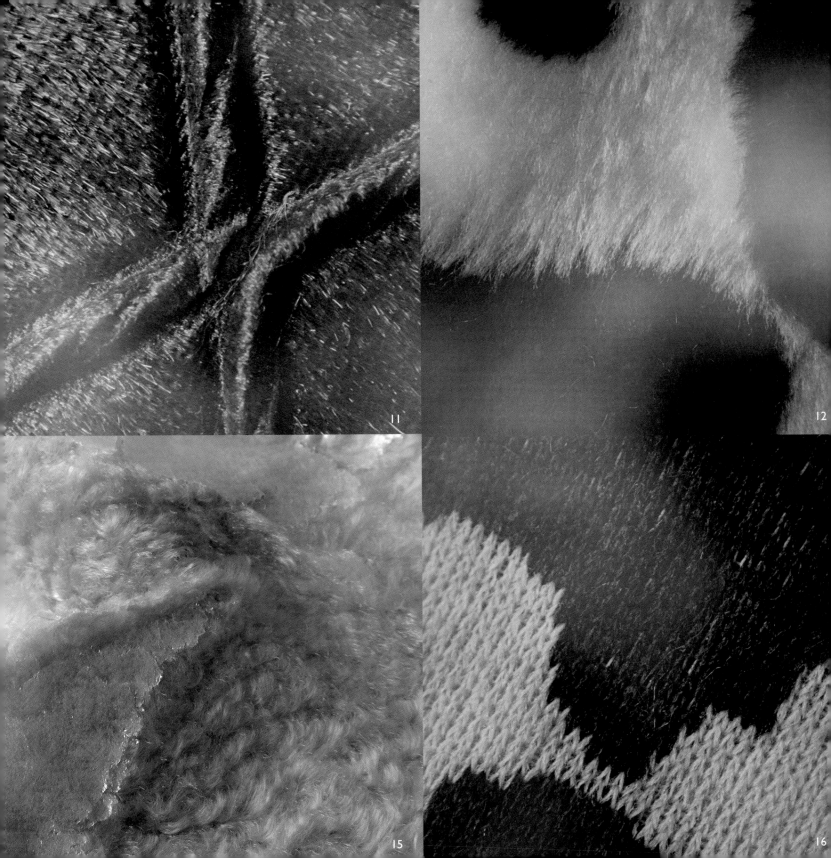

11

12

15

16

Fake fur

This is produced on pile machines. During the knitting of the plain stitches, fibres are air-propelled towards the needles. Tufts of fibres are then trapped in the interlinkages of the stitches and appear on the reverse jersey side. The yarns used for the knitting are often shrinkable. Sometimes a coating on the knit stitch side completes the securing of the fibres. Fur fabrics can be produced with multi-colour designs, as well as with fibres of very varied materials, sizes and appearance. They can then be partially heat-set or pressed to give them surface characteristics that resemble those of real furs.

Other, shorter pile fabric effects can also be produced using the plush jersey method.

At present, all of these textiles are difficult to produce on manual machines, especially in the gauges that are generally used. However, there is no reason why commercially bought textiles cannot be modified to produce new effects.

Page 274 – Plush jersey.
1, 2, 3, 4 – Relief patterned plush jersey produced by
selecting areas of reverse jersey (jacquard plush).
5 – Giant plush (or fringes) made in stripes.
6 – Plush jersey and four-colour jacquard.
7 – Two-colour plush and float jacquard.
8 – Two-colour plush jersey with relief.
Page 277: Fleecy fabric or polar fleece.
Page 278
9 – Fleecy fabric with brushing, effect side and reverse.
10 – Velvet or sheared plush jersey.
11 – Embossed velvet.
12 – Pile or fake fur knitted in two-colour jacquard;
effect side and reverse.
13, 14 – Pile.
15 – Pleating and bonding a film onto a pile fabric.
Page 280 – Fake fur.
Page 282 – Printed fake fur.

Conclusion and useful tips

In the knitting industry, technical improvements to knitting machines, along with developments in materials and treatments, have awakened huge creative potential, particularly at a tactile and visual level.

The suggestions for creating the effects, structures and motifs illustrated in this book should be regarded as pathways to progress that will keep opening up and will invigorate the creation of knitted textiles, whose applications are increasingly being extended beyond the field of clothing into the realms of the environment and industry. Among the many topics I have covered, here are some of the important elements that seem to offer the most interesting prospects for future development:

- the many different qualities of the yarns used.
- treatments and finishes incorporated into the yarn, both before and after knitting.
- casting on and casting off stitches at the start and end of a piece and anywhere within it.
- the potential to 'change gauge' without changing machine.
- changing the stitch size in one course.
- the ability to hold stitches out of action, at the same time continuing to work over the same wales, as a result of the development of new types of needle and the presser foot. These advances are making it much easier to produce three-dimensional pieces and structures that no longer have to be knitted just straight across but can be knitted in any direction.
- transfers that are becoming both faster and more complex, with introduction of segmented needlebeds that are much more mobile.
- the efficiency of the intarsia technique. Some machines are now able to use up to forty-eight different yarns in one course and, at the same time, can produce ever more complex stitch structures.
- knitting three-dimensional pieces with ribs, cable stitches, decreases, and so on.
- knitting complete seamless articles.
- the number of needlebeds, which has increased from two to three, four, five and more, thereby making it possible, while knitting a piece in the round, to add all kinds of details such as pockets, collars and rib edges.
- all aspects of the business that go unseen by customers, such as ergonomics and computerization, which are constantly evolving to boost equipment potential, facilitate user-friendliness and provide useful simulation tools so that the creative process takes aesthetics, quality and behaviour into account during production and in use.

Future improvements are sure to consolidate these achievements and lead to increased individual control of the movements of each needle. It can be expected that there will be some combination of weft knitting and warp knitting machines (as is already the case with Caperdoni machines) and perhaps even crochet, braiding, weaving, embroidery, needle punch and other machines.

It is also hoped that there will be an improvement in the skills of all parties involved in the chain, not just those of designers, stylists and technicians, but also those of decision-makers, marketing personnel and consumers, with whom there will have to be closer communication in order to maximize innovation. It is to be hoped that knitting will become increasingly attractive to artists and others as a means of self-expression.

Creating a weft-knitted fabric

A weft-knitted fabric is formed by interlinking a large number of stitches juxtaposed horizontally and forming courses or rows of stitches. These courses are superimposed to form columns of stitches called wales. One of the characteristics of this interlinking in knitting is that it unravels easily.

The stitches are produced using needles. In the knitting industry, the shape of the needles varies according to the machine. The latch needle was the type most commonly used in weft knitting machines. It is these needles that are used in domestic machines. Recent industrial knitting machines use compound needles. They have undergone many developments, as they considerably increase the potential of machines (in particular, they enable stitches to be kept out of action while continuing to knit).

For hand-knitting, the needles are cylindrical rods made from resin, metal or wood. In general, they have one tapered end, the other end being obstructed by a knob, so as to prevent the stitches from coming off. Other needles are pointed at both ends, for tubular knitting; they are also invaluable for experimentation, as they make it possible to knit in both directions.

Casting on stitches

Casting on is the operation that forms the very first stitches of a knitted fabric.

Old industrial knitting machines do not have the facility to cast on. Where this is the case, a technician places the stitches of any knitted fabric onto the needles, knits a number of courses and then one course with a contrasting auxiliary yarn, and then the definitive courses to begin the fabric. The entire

Above: Casting on stitches by hand
The first stitch is a slip-knot. Some distance from the end of the yarn held by the little finger, form a loop on the left thumb. The needle is in the right hand and the yarn from the ball, slips over the right index finger.

Slide the needle into the loop and let your hand pivot downwards.

Use the needle to bring through the yarn held by the little finger

Below: Forming the second stitch…

Release the loop held on the thumb, passing it over the needle.

The first stitch is formed by pulling moderately on the yarn with the left hand.

…and the following stitches (try to avoid over-tightening).

section below these is then removed by destroying or pulling on the separation yarn. This process is also used to quickly separate two panels.

On domestic machines, there are several ways of casting on, depending on the stitch structures you intend to create. Care is always required. To knit a classic plain fabric, on the first traverse of the carriage, knit only alternate needles; the other needles remain in position A. Then, a casting-on comb is hooked onto this yarn and the weights suspended. Then the needles out of action are moved to position B and, after increasing the tension dial slightly, the first course of the fabric is knitted.

In hand-knitting, there are also several ways of casting on, including the slipknot method (see previous pages), and the crochet method (see below).

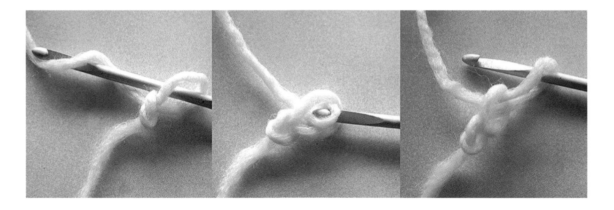

Moving a latch needle and forming a stitch

The movement of the needle is brought about by the butt of the needle coming up against the raising and descending cams. The latter are positioned under the carriage that travels over the needlebed(s). The cams are adjustable parts that activate and adjust the movement of the needles (front/back for flat-bed machines; high/low for circular machines) according to the different stitch structures that have been mechanically or electronically selected. Domestic machines have one cam system and feeder. Industrial machines have several feeders and are more efficient (up to six systems on current flat-bed machines and more than one hundred on circular machines).

A needlebed is a metal plate with parallel grooves (tricks) in which the needles are housed. Machines are usually equipped with one or two needlebeds. Today three, four or even five of them can be used to produce complex structures such as ribbed seamless articles, which are three dimensional.

Yarn guides are also essential parts for distributing the yarn to the needles. On domestic machines, there are two yarn guides secured to the carriage. On recent industrial machines, the yarn guides are independent and can be very numerous (16, 28, 32), making it possible to work with many yarns on one, two or three different panels.

By removing the front part of the carriage and moving it slowly over the needlebed, it is possible to observe the needles as they work:

- taking up/yarn feeding: the needle receives the yarn in its hook.
- dropping/knock-over: after taking up the yarn, the needle draws back, bringing the yarn with it. It passes through the stitch from the previous course which passes over the needle, while closing its latch, and drops off, 'falling' on top of the stitch of the previous course.
- forming: in the meantime the new stitch is being formed.

These terms are non-standard. They indicate the indistinguishable stages of the movements of the needle and the yarn while a stitch is being formed.

There are four key positions of the needles on the bed:

- position A: the needles are out of action.
- position B: the needles are knitting plain stitches.
- position C: the needles are selected to knit a design (or in position for intarsia).
- position D: the needles are out of action in areas while others are working.

The concept of gauge refers to the distance between two needles. Not all machine manufacturers use the same numbering system. The most commonly used domestic machines correspond to an English gauge of 4.5 (this is the number of needles per inch, i.e. 25.4 mm) and to a Swiss gauge of 56 (this is the distance in tenths of a millimetre between the axis of two adjacent needles, i.e. 5.6 mm). This is a fairly large gauge.

Other examples:

- extremely fine English gauge 32 = Swiss gauge 8 (or 0.8 mm between axes).
- fine English gauge 18 = Swiss gauge 14 (or 1.4 mm between axes).
- very heavy English gauge 2.5 = Swiss gauge 100 (or 1 cm between axes).

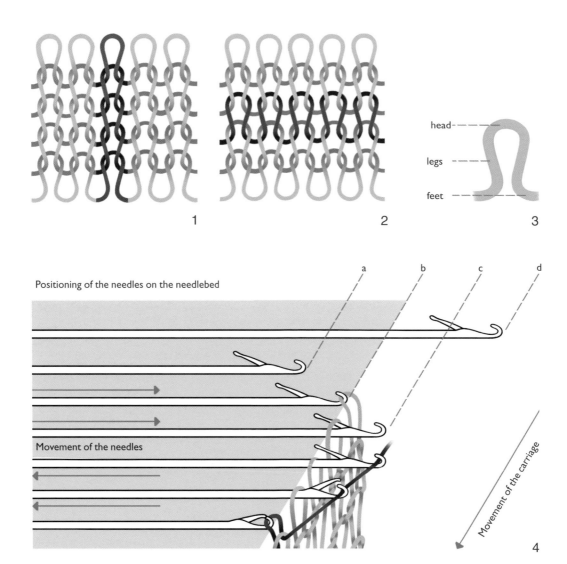

1   2   3

head
legs
feet

Positioning of the needles on the needlebed

a   b   c   d

Movement of the needles

Movement of the carriage

4

Multi-gauge machines can now be used in a more flexible manner. It is possible to change gauge to knit different articles. It is also possible, in the same piece, to use yarns of very different count such as, for example, 8 gauge needles and 6 and 12 gauge knit (see the section on fully-fashioned fabrics in chapter 13).

The size of the stitch is also dependent on the tension or stitch dial setting. It is the setting of the lowering cams that changes the distance covered by the needles. The yarn used therefore varies in length and the knitted fabric varies in density from loose to tight. At present the notion of tension is often replaced by that of length of yarn used. Some industrial machines have the facility to work with very accurate changes in stitch length along the same course of stitches, but on domestic machines this is not mechanically possible. To produce some stitch structures it is necessary to work without the carriage. The needles are manually knitted by pushing them to the correct position after taking up the yarn.

Another essential setting is the tension of the yarn. This is adjusted by the pressure exerted by the yarn grip and the feeding mechanism. A great deal of care is required when threading, positioning the cones and supervising the yarn feeding.

In hand-knitting, a change in gauge and tension is made by using thinner or thicker needles. To produce changes along the same row, simply wind the yarn two or more times around the needle (without tightening). On the next row, only one 'yarn over' is knitted, and the others are released.

Casting off stitches

The term casting off is used to describe binding off the stitches.

In the knitting industry, this was usually achieved by manually sewing or by overlocking. Recent machines bind off stitches once the panels are finished, though they may also do this anywhere on the fabric, which means that highly complex fancy structures, finishes and shapes can be created.

On manual machines, if a neat edge is required, the stitches are bound off using a hand tool. At a selvedge, on the carriage side, the first stitch is transferred onto the next one and these two stitches are knitted together by feeding the yarn into the hook of the needle and then pushing the needle back into its initial position. This operation is then repeated over the entire course. Then the yarn is cut, passed through the last stitch and pulled tight.

For sampling, it is preferable to save time spent on casting on and particularly casting off. The samples can be knitted continuously and then separated, by locking the stitches with an overlocker, sewing machine or an adhesive in the absence of a more suitable method of presentation.

In hand-knitting, casting off stitches is done by (separately) knitting the first two stitches, (*) then pass the first stitch over the second using the other needle, and finally let it drop off the needle. Then knit the next stitch (*) and repeat from (*) to (*) until all the stitches have been done (see the photographs opposite).

Casting on and casting off are also used during the knitting process to produce a range of surface effects, and to create special structures within the knitted fabric (see chapters 2 and 13).

Diagrammatic representations

Schematic notations that represent the yarn movements during knitting are the standard means of recording the process of constructing a particular knitted fabric, and are used to instruct the technicians responsible for turning the designs into finished pieces.

	needle in working position
●	needle missed (held stitch)
✕	needle out of action (no stitch)
Ω	stitch on the back needlebed
℧	stitch on the front needlebed
⅄	tuck on the back needlebed
⋎	tuck on the front needlebed

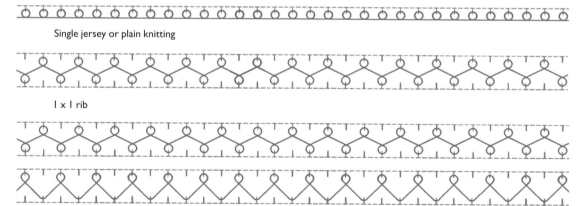

Single jersey or plain knitting

1 x 1 rib

Half cardigan or beaded rib

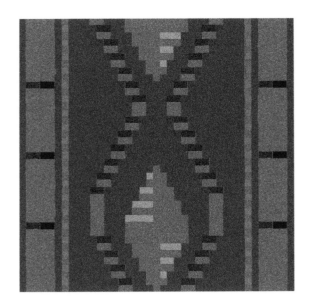

Programming of the Shima Seiki industrial knitting machine

- front bed loop
- back bed loop
- front bed loop with transfer one position to the left
- front bed loop with transfer one position to the right
- front bed loop, crossed under
- front bed loop crossed over
- back bed loop, crossed under
- tuck loop on front

Stitch simulation on computer screen

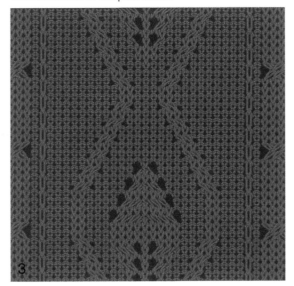

Knitted sample

Graph representation

This non-standard representation allows the stitch structures to be visualized, and makes charting the design for knitting by machine easier. Any basic symbols or colours can be chosen, depending on the particular knitting structure you wish to create. It is essential to accompany a stitch graph with a key to the symbols used. For example, patterns published by Phildar state in brackets the terms used in hand-knitting.

No stitch

| Knit stitch on the right side or face

—   Purl stitch on the right side

o   Gap (or tuck at the base of a new wale)

Ɐ   Held stitch or slipped stitch, float at back

V   Held stitch float in front

∩   Tuck loop

⋉   Two knit stitches crossed to the right

⋉   One knit stitch crossed to the right over a purl stitch

⋊   Two knit stitches crossed to the left over a purl stitch

⋊⋉   Four knit stitches crossed two over two to the right

⋇   Held stitch crossed to the right over a purl stitch

╱   Transfer of one knit stitch to the right

╲   Transfer of one purl stitch to the left

⟨   Two stitches knitted together slanting to the right

⟩   Two stitches knitted together slanting to the left (slip 1 knit 1, pass slipped stitch over)

⋏   Transfer of two stitches, one to the right and one to the left onto a third stitch in the centre (three knit stitches knitted together, the second on top)

⋩   Three stitches purled together and slanted to the left

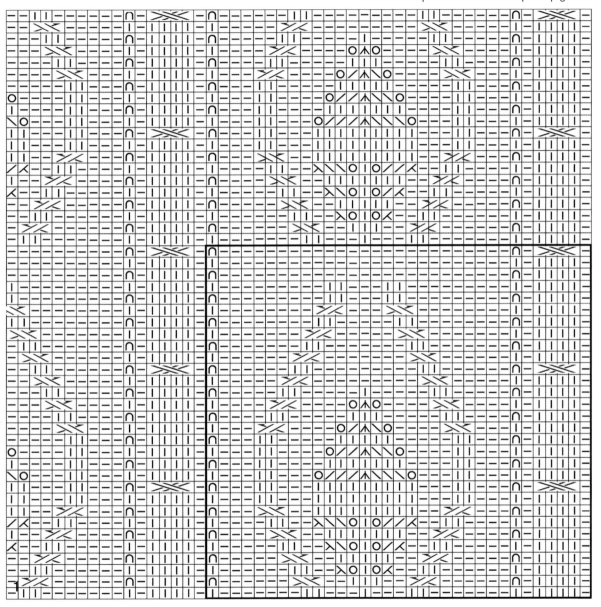

The stitches are represented on a graph that shows the right side of the final fabric. Each cell of the grid corresponds to one stitch. The symbols in each box are graphic representations of the way in which each stitch is knitted. One complete repeat of the design motif is indicated by the heavier framed box, which can be repeated horizontally and vertically to create an all-over pattern. The stitches are counted from right to left, and the pattern rows from bottom to top. On a single-bed knitting machine (back needlebed), the fabric is only visible from the purl or reverse jersey side. Consequently, the direction of the symbols has to be reversed: a stitch slanting to the right on the graph must be transferred to the left on the machine and vice versa.

That's all – now all you have to do is go out and be creative. Even beginners can be inspired by these images to turn their own dreams into reality. So what are you waiting for? Start knitting!

Glossary

All-over   Design motif repeated over the entire surface of a fabric.

Aran knitting   A type of textured knitting that contains racked and transferred stitches.

Bar   In knitted goods, a stripe formed by a manufacturing fault.

Batt or wadding   Short textile fibres that are tangled together.

Beam   A cylinder on which the warp threads are wound during the manufacture of both warp knitted and woven fabrics.

Bouclé   Fancy yarn incorporating loops. Fabric knitted or woven from bouclé yarns.

Bourrelet see **ripple**

Braids and trimmings   Narrow bands of various materials, made with a range of techniques, designed as decoration.

Brushing   Treatment that raises the hairs of the fibres within the cloth, covering the underlying structure of the fabric and giving a fluffy texture.

Cable stitch   In weft knitting, crossings of several stitches repeated at intervals in the same wales.

Cam   Triangular pieces of metal (one raising cam and two lowering cams) found under the carriage of a knitting machine. When they are positioned on the needlebed, the cams act upon the needle butts and determine their movement.

Cam track   Assembly of parts underneath the carriage of the knitting machine, which allows the formation of tuck stitches.

Carriage   The carriage is one of the principal parts of a knitting machine. It carries the raising and lowering cams and holds the mechanical apparatus for knitting.

Centring   Folding of a fabric selvedge to selvedge.

Chain   The basic stitch element in hand crochet. In warp knitting, one of the warp threads that makes up the fabric structure.

Chain stitch   A sewing and embroidery stitch. It is used in many areas, particularly in packaging, where its ability to unravel quickly enables two elements to be held together then separated easily.

Chainette   Fancy yarn consisting of either a single chain of stitches or a small number of stitches in tubular form.

Chart   The representation of a knitted pattern on graph paper.

Chenille   Fancy yarn with a velvety texture.

Chevron   Zig-zag pattern.

Chiné   Describes fancy yarns made of different coloured fibres or of several materials that react differently to dyeing. Also describes the fabrics made with these yarns.

Coating Deposit of a layer of chemicals on a fabric to modify its characteristics, such as waterproofing.

Cone Conical support on which yarn is wound.

Co-ordinates Fabrics designed to be used together but with different characteristics.

Cord Very small tubular knitting.

Cornely Originally the inventor of an embroidery machine that utilizes a hooked needle, and now a term for embroidery made on Cornely machines. The basic stitches are chain stitch and loop stitch or pile (open chain). Various accessories allow the application of fancy braids onto a backing, which may or may not be removed.

Count see **yarn count**

Covered Describes fancy yarns made up of several elements of which one is used as a covering.

Crepe Describes a type of crinkled yarn or a fabric with a crumpled texture, created with crepe yarns and/or using stitch structure.

Crepon Fabric with a grainy uneven texture.

Cut and sew Term used to denote garments cut out and manufactured from lengths of cloth or from panels.

Cutting A sample piece from a width of fabric.

Denier see **yarn count**

Density This term describes the consistency of a fabric. It is the result of the yarn count, fibre, and the texture of the yarn used, the gauge and the stitch dial settings or tension.

Double bed Knitting machines with two sets of needles facing each other.

Double-face fabrics In knitting, these are reversible fabrics whose sides may be either identical or different, self-coloured or jacquard.

Double moss stitch In weft knitting, double moss stitch (or seed stitch) is a basic purl fabric structure. It consists of one plain and one purl stitch (one by one rib), alternating every two courses.

Dupion Describes fancy yarns that are irregular and variable in size, particularly silk.

Edging or trimming Finishings such as cuffs and collars, made during the knitting of a garment or sewn on during the making up of the pieces.

Effect yarn Fancy spun yarn that enlivens the fabric surface.

Eight lock Weft-knitting machines that enable the knitting of interlock fabrics and derivatives. The term also describes the fabrics themselves.

Elasticity The ability of a fibre to regain its original form after being stretched.

Embroidery   Decoration sewn on to a textile backing (which may eventually disintegrate; not to be confused with lace).

Extensibility   The ability of certain materials to stretch.

Fabrics   A fabric is a surface made from yarn in which the enmeshing conforms to a range of techniques. There are:

Fabrics with looped yarns: weft knitting, warp knitting.

Fabrics with straight yarns: weaving, tapestry, carpets, terry towelling, gauze.

Fabrics with multi-directional yarns: tulle, lace, guipure.

Fabrics with three-way yarns: braids, basketry.

Geo-textiles or technical textiles: used for filtration, drainage, waterproofing, stabilization and soil reinforcement.

Non-woven fabrics: felt, plastic films, coated fabrics, bonded fibres.

Face or right side   This term is generally used to denote the most interesting side of a fabric. In weft knitting, reversible structures that are the same on both sides are termed fabrics with no wrong side.

Fashioned   Fabric with a design that is obtained through structural shaping. In weft knitting, garment pieces obtained by knitting to shape. See **fully-fashioned**.

Finishings   The range of treatments and processes that can be applied to fabrics (or garments) at the end of production. Also refers to details that complete a made-up garment – edgings, fringes, braids, etc.

Fléchage see **partial knitting**

Fleck   Fancy yarn containing small loose fibres in multiple colours.

Fleece   These are soft and supple fabrics. After knitting, the fabrics are brushed on one or both sides and sometimes also sheared in parts.

Fleecy yarn   In weft knitting, a fluffy yarn inlaid between knitted stitches then brushed.

Float   In weft knitting, these are threads that pass horizontally when certain needles are out of action, or are momentarily missed when knitting slip-stitch patterns. They are also found in some jacquards, and in inlaid fabrics.

Float stitch   Term used to describe fabrics with dropped stitches and floats created on the knitting machine by missing out needles.

Flocking   Application of short textile fibres (through printing of adhesive) onto a supporting fabric. A velvet effect covers some or all of the surface, according to the type of design used.

Fraying   Tearing or distressing of a fabric.

Fringe   Finishing for a woven or knitted fabric. The fringe is also a braid trimming found in passementerie.

Fully fashioned or fashioned   This term is used to describe knitwear in which panels are shaped like pattern pieces. They are made by decreasing or increasing stitches during the knitting.

Garter stitch   In weft knitting, garter stitch is a basic purl fabric structure. It consists of alternately one course knit, one course purl. Both sides of the fabric are the same.

Gauge   Refers to the distance between two needles, and therefore, by extension, to the size of knitted loops. English gauge is defined by the number of needles per inch (25.4 mm), and Swiss gauge by the distance in tenths of a millimetre between the axes of two adjacent needles.

Gimp   Describes a fancy marl yarn with a small-scale wavy structure.

Grainy   Describes fancy yarns and fabrics with an irregular rough surface.

Hank or skein   A quantity of unsupported wound yarn.

Held or slipped stitches   These stitch structures are formed with needle loops that are held and elongated over several courses during which other needles are knitting.

History of knitting   The knitting industry is relatively young. Up to the end of the sixteenth century, knitting was only done by hand. The invention of hand-knitting cannot be dated with any certainty, but probably occurred more than a thousand years ago. It may have been imported from the Far East at the beginning of the present era. Many historical works refer to the importance of the craft in the Middle Ages: it was used for reliquaries, gloves, bonnets, tunics made of silk and cotton. An English curate, William Lee, devised the first machine for knitting in 1589. But it was not until 1656 that Colbert founded the first hosiery factory in France. In 1853, Matthew Townsend invented the latch needle; its semi-automatic operation enabled the construction of knitting machines that were much simpler to operate. Since its creation, the knitting machine has never stopped developing. Now, programmable automatic machines are extremely versatile; each new model has features which are increasingly sophisticated.

Hosiery   This term denotes both the industry and the manufacturing process of knitted garments (particularly underwear and legwear), or knitwear made by the cut and sew method from knitted fabric.

Inlay   In weft knitted fabrics, the inlay yarn is held in place by the feet of the stitch loops in single jersey fabrics, and lays between the face and reverse wales in ribbed fabrics.

Inlay warp knitting   see **weft insertion**

Intarsia A 'jacquard' knitted on a plain jersey or rib base or using a variety of structures, comprising different yarns in the same course. The yarns only appear in the area where they are used in the design, and both right side and wrong side look the same.

Interlock Interlock fabrics are made on double-bed machines and on eight-lock machines in very fine gauge. They comprise interlinked rib structures (1 x 1 or 2 x 2 ribs). Derivatives include fabrics with tucks and slip stitches, in self colour or stripes. The needles are directly opposite each other.

Jacquard This term derives from Joseph-Marie Jacquard, inventor of a mechanical process that enables the creation of woven and knitted fabrics incorporating patterns. It is also used to denote the fabrics themselves. In weft knitting there are two forms: structured jacquards and colour jacquards. The latter can be made in different ways:

Blister jacquard: On the right side, the design appears in relief with background stitches in the base colour. On the reverse side the surface is single colour self-patterned.

Double jacquard with birdseye backing: Birdseye jacquard has a piqué quality. On the reverse, needles are half gauged, and stitches are knitted alternately every two courses, creating a lighter weight fabric.

Double jacquard with striper backing: This jacquard and its derivatives are made on a double-bed machine. On the striped backing all the needles are in use on each pass of the carriage.

Double-face or reversible jacquard: The design appears on both sides of the fabric, sometimes in positive and negative form, sometimes with two different patterns.

Fancy jacquard: Some jacquards may have textural effects in certain areas, such as racking and transfer.

Jersey jacquard: This jacquard is made on single-bed machines. Knit loops on the face of the fabric in two, three or four colours in the course are alternated according to the design. On the reverse, the yarns that are not knitted, float.

Transfer jacquard: The stitches of the pattern are selected, knitted and transferred to the back bed. They appear on a ground of striped reverse jersey or of floats, tuck stitches or purl fabric, in two or more colours.

Jaspé Describes a fancy yarn made of mixed fibres twisted together. This uneven quality can also be obtained through dyeing. The surface of the resulting fabric is reminiscent of the coloured stone called jasper.

Kemp Describes a rough-looking type of yarn incorporating a few or many hairs of a different colour and texture to the main yarn.

Knitting up   Manual re-knitting of dropped loops.

Knock-over or cast-off   After having collected the yarn from the feeder, the needle draws back, holding the yarn in its hook. The yarn is then pulled through the loop from the previous course, which passes over the needle whose latch has now closed, and the old stitch drops off, falling on top of the stitch in the previous course.

Knop   Small knots in some fancy yarns. In weft-knitted fabrics, a small raised cluster within the structure, usually created by multiple tuck loops.

Knopped   Describes fabrics and fancy yarns with knots of excess fibres called knops, at irregular intervals, in self-colour or multicolour.

Lace   Fabric with both transparent and opaque areas. It is made by various techniques: bobbin (hand-made) lace, machine lace, warp knitting, weft knitting.

Laddering   Term used in weft knitting when a stitch drops and unravels the whole length of the piece.

Laminating   A process that involves glueing or bonding two or three surfaces together.

Lay   Width of a cloth from one selvedge to the other.

Links-links   see **purl fabric**

Looped yarn fabrics   These are textiles made by the intermeshing of loops. There are two types: weft knitted and warp knitted.

Lurex   Brand name of a fancy yarn made from slit-film laminate of plasticized metal.

Lycra   Brand name of an elastic fibre: elastane, composed primarily of polyurethane.

Marker   Mark made on the selvedge to signify a fault.

Marl   Describes a fancy yarn composed of two or more yarns, usually of different colours, twisted together, such as a crepe yarn.

Materials used for textiles

Textiles of animal origin: These are made from the hair of animals or the secretions of insects: sheep (wool), goat (mohair, cashmere), rabbit (angora), camel, llama, vicuna, alpaca, silkworms, spiders (silk) or shells.

Textiles of chemical origin: Artificial and synthetic textiles are obtained by processes of varying complexity from different base materials of plant, animal or mineral origin. A first-level transformation will give for example: viscose, acetate, glass fibre, metallic yarns, metallized plastic yarns. More complex transformations are used to produce polyamide, polyester, acrylic, polyurethane or polyolefin.

Textiles of mineral origin: Asbestos, metals, peat.

Textiles of natural origin: These are obtained by physical and mechanical transformation of natural fibres without altering their composition.

Textiles of plant origin: These are made from the seeds, stems, leaves and sap of plants, and include cotton, kapok, linen, hemp, jute, ramie, sisal, coconut and rubber.

Mercerization   Treatment that gives a smooth and shiny finish to a yarn, usually cotton.

Mesh   Used to denote all types of product (textile or not) that consist of open loops.

Mesh fabric   Fabric (which does not unravel) also called tricot when made on warp-knitting machines.

Metric count (Nm)   This is the most frequently used unit for defining the count of a yarn. It indicates the number of kilometres of yarn that weigh a kilogram. The larger the number, the finer the yarn.

Milano   A structure in weft knitting made on a rib machine, consisting of one course circular knitting, one course 1 x 1 rib.

Half milano: On one needlebed, all the needles knit, on the other needlebed all the stitches are held, alternating with one course 1 x 1 rib.

Moss stitch   In weft knitting, moss stitch is a basic purl fabric structure. It consists of one plain and one purl stitch (1 x 1 rib), alternating every course.

Needlebed   On a knitting machine, the needlebed is the metal plate containing grooves (or tricks) in which the needles travel. Machines may have one or two needlebeds according to their production function. Some flat-bed machines have four or five.

Ondulé   Describes a yarn with an exaggerated wavy effect.

Openwork   Fabric with decorative holes or gaps, which can be woven, knitted or embroidered. In weft knitting it is made by transferring stitches to adjacent needles. See also **lace**.

Panel   A fabric of fixed dimensions.

Partial knitting or *fléchage*   The technique of putting needles out of action in one part of the fabric, while the others keep knitting. This enables fully-fashioned knitwear to be made, as well as many other striking stitch effects.

Patchwork   An assembly of different fabrics sewn together. By extension, any design composed of different materials, prints and structures juxtaposed together.

Piece length   The entire meterage between the start and finish of a cloth piece.

Piqué   Small relief pattern created from different stitches in weft knitting.

Placement pattern   This is a single design or motif positioned on a fabric or garment. It can be in contrast colour, fibre, or structure, made in woven, knitted or lace fabrics, or embroidered or printed.

Plain fabric   see **single jersey**

Plating   This is the simultaneous knitting of two different yarns (in colour, fibre or count), one of which is visible on the face and the other on the reverse of single jersey. On double-face fabrics, one yarn is visible on both faces and the other is present inside, only revealed if stitches are removed.

Pleats   In weft knitting, pleats are made on double-bed fine-gauge machines by an arrangement of needles for wide rib or full needle rib. Some pleats can be varied with rib jacquard and relief effects. There are accordion pleats, box pleats, and knife pleats. Very fine-gauge knitted fabrics can be pleated (regularly or irregularly) by heat pressing.

Plush   Single jersey plush fabric is made by knitting with two yarns simultaneously – one is used as the base yarn (which is often elastic), while the other forms loops on the reverse side. It can be completely or partially covered in loops, knitted in self colour or in two-colour jacquard.

Polar fleece   A type of fabric made by weaving, warp knitting or weft knitting. In the latter case, it is made from plush jersey. Both sides of the fabric are brushed.

Pompom (or pompon)   Small 'puffball' made of short lengths of yarn, used as a trimming.

Presser foot or plate   This is a solid apparatus, part of the carriage, which enables the stitches of jersey or rib fabrics to be held down without the use of weights or a take-down bar, which elongates the knitting.

Prototype   Fabric sample or reference garment for production.

Punto di Roma   This is a structure in weft knitting made on a rib machine. It has two interlock 1 × 1 rib courses.

Purl fabric or links-links   These are weft-knitted structures in which certain wales contain both face and reverse loops, i.e. knit and purl stitches.

Quilted   A textile made with two fabrics enclosing a bulky material (such as wadding) and held together by stitching through the layers.

Racking   The operation of displacing one needlebed in relation to the other.

Repeat   Height and width dimensions of a pattern that is designed to repeat all over.

Rib   In weft knitting, ribs consist of wales of plain and purl stitches. The various types include:
Derby rib: These fabrics consist of groups of plain and purl stitch wales of variable widths, particularly 6 × 3 rib.

Fancy rib: These ribs may be made of bands of knit or purl stitches of varying widths, with patterns of stripes, purl stitches, floats, transfer stitches, with or without racking, or a combination of many different possibilities.

Full cardigan or fisherman's rib: This rib is made in two stages repeated throughout the length: one course of alternate plain and tuck stitch, one course of alternate tuck and plain stitches (i.e. the opposite way to the previous course).

Full needle rib: All needles of both needlebeds, racked a half pitch, knit on every course.

Half cardigan or beaded rib: This rib is made in two stages: one course of I x I rib, and one course of alternate plain and tuck stitches. The two courses are repeated throughout the length.

Ribbed   Fabric made of coarse or fine ribs.

Ridged   Knitted fabric with weft-ways (horizontal) relief effects, such as patterns of ripples (*bourrelets*), stripes or 'welts' of purl stitches.

Ripple or *bourrelet*   Ripples or *bourrelets* are created by knitting several additional courses of single jersey (or jersey jacquard) on one side of a double bed ribbed (or double jacquard) fabric.

Ruched or puckered   A relief textured fabric surface created by specific stitch structures.

Sample   A small quantity of a yarn or fabric, used for assessment purposes.

Self-coloured fabric   This term often describes fabrics in only one colour, without textural effects; but in the knitting industry it means all textiles made without jacquard patterning.

Self-patterned   Fabric with subtle patterning.

Selvedge   Closed side edges of a fabric.

Single jersey or plain fabric   The basic stitch structure in weft knitting. It is made on flat-bed knitting machines with a single needlebed, and on double-bed machines in circular or semi-circular knitting, or on circular knitting machines in tubular knitted fabric. Jersey consists of plain knit loops, endlessly repeated across the whole surface of the fabric. The two sides look completely different: these are called the face (knit) and reverse (purl) sides of the fabric (or right side and wrong side).

Shadow lace   see **thread lace**

Shrinkage   A decrease in the dimensions of a yarn or cloth.

Skein   see **hank**

Slitting   Cutting a float or tubular knitted fabric along its length to create 'open width' fabric.

Slub   Describes a fancy yarn that varies in size along its length, with heavier parts in the form of slubs. Also refers to fabric made of such yarns.

Snarl   Describes a fancy yarn with large or small 'protrusions' formed by twisted loops.

Spinning   The entire process of transforming textile fibres into yarn.

Spotted   Describes yarns and fabrics with coloured scattered marks or spots.

Stitch   A single loop of yarn. It comprises the *head* at the top, the *foot* at the bottom, and in between these, the *legs*.

Stitch density or tension   In knitting, the number of wales and courses in a given area.

Stitch forming   This term indicates the step immediately after the knock-over, during which the new stitch is formed.

Stitch setting   The stitch setting corresponds to the length of the stitch. Regulation of the dial controls the stitch density of the knitted fabric. In fact, this concept is characterized by the length of yarn used.

Stitch structure   Term denoting the manner in which the yarns intermesh in weft-knitted fabrics.

Stretch   A characteristic of extensible fabrics made with elastane yarns.

Take-down   On weft-knitting machines, the fabric has a tendency to lift up during knitting. An arrangement of comb and weights or a take-down bar avoids this inconvenience. Some recent machines are able to vary the take-down pressure on the fabric.

Tex   *see* **yarn count**

Thread lace or shadow lace   In weft knitting, this is a lace effect obtained without transferring stitches. This fabric is made in jacquard with one transparent or very fine yarn and one opaque yarn. It is often called fishnet.

Transfer stitch   The transfer of a stitch loop to a nearby needle.

Treatments and finishes   During and after their manufacture, textiles can receive treatments that may change their look, handle, or other properties. Possible finishes include: bleaching, dyeing, printing (flocking, devoré), coating, embroidery, brushing, glazing, starching, cracking, degumming, calandering, embossing, moiré, felting, shirring, milling, mercerizing, pressing, singeing, shearing, shrink-resistant, waterproofing, water-repellant, anti-creasing, mothproofing, flameproofing, flame retardant, insect resistant, decatizing, anti-static, anti-bacterial, easy-care, anti-rot.

Tricot   Term used to describe certain warp knitting machines and fabrics. See **mesh fabric**.

Trimming   *see* **edging**

Tubular   Fabric in the form of a tube. In weft knitting, these fabrics can be made on double-bed flat machines, and on circular machines.

Tuck   In knitting a tuck, the yarn is collected by the needle without being knitted through.

Velvet   Fabric with a short pile or loops. Various techniques are used to produce different forms of velvet in weaving, warp knitting and weft knitting.

Wadding   Stuffing enclosed between two fabrics. See also **batt**.
Wale   One column of stitches in a piece of weft knitting.

Warp knitting   Warp-knitted fabrics are formed from warps consisting of vertical chains of loops that intermesh across the width of the knitting. Warp knits do not unravel easily.
Weft   In weaving, the yarn that is perpendicular to the warp.
Weft insertion or inlay warp knitting   Warp-knitted fabrics in which one or more weft yarns are laid in to the fabric and trapped between the loops of the warp chains.
Weft knitting   Weft-knitted fabrics are created from successive loops repeated across the width of the knitting, each of which intermeshes with a preceeding loop forming the entire length.

Yarn count or count   This indicates the size of a yarn, and states the relationship between length and weight. The finer the yarn, the higher the number. The most frequently used unit is the metric number (symbol Nm), It shows the number of kilometres of yarn in one kilogram weight. Tex is an international unit for yarn count based on the decimal system. It corresponds to the weight in grammes of 1,000 metres of yarn. Denier (den) is the weight in grammes of 9,000 metres of yarn.
Yarn types
Cabled yarn: Yarn made from several yarns of which one or more is plied or cabled, then twisted together.
Covered yarn: Yarn made from one or more yarns wrapped around a core yarn.
Fancy yarn: A yarn whose appearance is significantly different from a classic yarn: bouclé, knop, chiné, chenille, crepe, dupion, fleck, gimp, wavy, speckled, coated, covered, slub, crimped, printed, marl, irisé, jaspé, space dyed, woven, knitted, snarl.
Fibre-spun yarn: Yarn composed of short fibres held together by twisting, bonding, or another process.
Flat yarn or slit film: A continuous strip made by slitting: may be made from paper, raffia, cellophane or metallized plastic.
Folded or plied yarn: Yarn made up of several singles yarns twisted together.
Monofilament yarn: Yarn consisting of one single filament with or without twist such as silk or nylon.
Multifilament yarn: Yarn consisting of many filaments with or without twist.
Singles yarn: Single-ply yarn spun from fibres, multifilament yarn, or flat yarn, with or without twist.
Texturized yarn: Synthetic yarn with or without twist or elasticity. It is given a bulky texture by friction, looping or crimping.

Acknowledgments

My special thanks to Maurice Bardon, head of research and development at Établissements Terrot in Paris, to Dominique Chocu-Rispal, director of the research office at Établissements Synertex in Port-Brillet, and to Jean-Pierre Matthelié, head of research and development at the I.F.T.H. (Institut Français Textile Habillement) in Troyes, for having agreed to read through this book and give me their comments and suggestions.

I also wish to thank the following companies: Bel Maille, Billon, Houlé Dentelles, Jabouley, New Maille Stop and France Tissu Maille, as well as the Lineapiu mill in Florence, Italy, for having supplied me with knitted samples.

Finally, my thanks to Céline Tellier and Gilles Tellier for their help throughout the making of this book.